Healing *beyond* Betrayal

Marriage Built *to* Last:
Healing *beyond* Betrayal

JENNIFER KARINA

Marriage Built to Last: Healing Beyond Betrayal

Copyright © 2015 Jennifer Karina

All Rights Reserved.

ISBN: 978-1-937455-231

Published by;

P.O. Box 58411,
Raleigh, NC 27658
U.S.A.
info@integritypublishers.org

Publishing Consultants:

info@publishing-institute.org
www.publishing-institute.org

All rights reserved. No portion of this book may be reproduced or transmitted in any form or by any means without the written permission of the author or Publisher.

I dedicate this book to all married couples.

*Beloved, you have committed yourselves
to each other in marriage.*

The Church of Christ understands marriage to be

in the will of God,

the union of a man and a woman,

for better, for worse,

for richer, for poorer,

in sickness and in health,

to love and to cherish,

'til parted by death.

May you thrive in your relationships.

Contents

Foreword ix
Preface xi
Acknowledgements xiii

Chapter One
A Nasty Surprise 1

Chapter Two
In the Shadow of the Ex 11

Chapter Three
Impossible to Please 27

Chapter Four
Hidden Wealth 37

Chapter Five
No Dirty Laundry in Public 47

Chapter Six
Someone Else Has My Back 57

Chapter Seven
Kids Causing Troubled Waters 67

Chapter Eight
No Longer the Man He Was 77

Chapter Nine
Worse Than Soap Opera 85

Chapter Ten
The Woman in His Mind 97
Conclusion 107
References 111

Foreword

It is a great honour for me to write the foreword of my wife's second book, *Marriage Built to Last: Healing beyond Betrayal*. I do it gladly, with a deep sense of pride as her husband and friend. A great deal of investment has been made into making this book a reality. I have watched Jennie labour year after year in pursuit of her purpose and passion to help others build strong, lasting, and thriving relationships. She has done this through various forums, the media, and the power of the written word.

Healing beyond Betrayal is a precious book, straight from the heart. It is based on real-life situations of couples who have experienced pain, frustration, and hurt but have graciously chosen to share their lives with others who can learn from them to avoid similar pitfalls. Or if damage has already been done, for them to know that all is not lost. There is hope for these couples to heal and to thrive, if both parties are willing to work on their relationship. Jennie is committed to helping individuals enjoy a marriage built to last. Her vision is to encourage would-be-married couples to do so with the right understanding and to influence those already in marriage to cherish their relationships.

Jennie believes that people cannot consider themselves successful by doing well in only one aspect of their lives. If their families are neglected, this will adversely affect their status and, consequently, their careers, reputations, and spiritual lives. She thinks that the institution of marriage is under attack and must be protected. She also acknowledges that marriage is a gift from God and a core value of humankind, which should be

Foreword

harnessed, treasured, and protected always. I am one blessed beneficiary of her vision and determination to see every marriage happy and fulfilled. I can confidently say that she knows what she is talking about.

Healing beyond Betrayal is a great book, a worthy investment. You will be greatly enriched by reading it.

Bob Karina
Founder and Chairman
Faida Investment Bank
June 2015

Preface

Marriage is a gift from God. It should be harnessed, treasured, and protected always. Marriage is a lifetime commitment and must not be taken lightly. I have been married for more than thirty years and hold the view that it is beautiful. It should be enjoyed and not endured, and everybody should endeavour for a "marriage built to last".

Every day, many couples tie the knot in lavish weddings, in the hope of enjoying lifetime unions. Unfortunately, even before they can celebrate their first anniversaries, some of those marital relationships fall apart, and society loses another building block in its structure. Traditionally, marriages are supposed to last for life regardless of quality, but today's generation does not have the patience to wait for them to transform over time. They can end abruptly, shattering hearts.

Since the successful launch of *Marriage Built to Last*, I have realised that we need to be continuously proactive in enhancing the quality of marriages, through coaching and counselling. Most people put great consideration and effort into the wedding preparations but neglect to do so for the lifelong marital journey. They end up in the deep end of the pool, without knowing how to swim.

This new book, *Marriage Built to Last: Healing beyond Betrayal*, is a response to the stories of despair. It is a collection of real-life stories—shared with people's consent but disguised to protect their identities—accompanied by commentaries based on Biblical principles, research, and my personal insights.

Preface

Healing beyond Betrayal takes you on a familiar journey—yours or somebody else's. Either way, I hope it can support you or that other person and make a difference in your lives. It can help you identify behaviours that may damage your marriage. It can also assist you in developing healthy means to deal with marital challenges and conscious steps to meet your spouse's and your needs in an intimate, personal way.

I trust that this book will enrich your relationship and help you as a couple enjoy a greater degree of love and unity. You will recognise that you are not alone; several other people have gone through/are going through similar difficulties as you are. In spite of all that, get up and walk. Find your healing. Be inspired, encouraged, and empowered.

Live, love, and thrive because you deserve it!

Jennie Karina
June 2015

Acknowledgements

This book is a testimony of God's faithfulness—all glory and honour to Him as the Giver of every good and perfect gift, including marriage.

I offer special appreciation to the individuals who gave their written consent to have their stories included in *Marriage Built to Last: Healing beyond Betrayal*. You allowed yourselves to be vulnerable for the sake of others, so they could learn, grow, and glow for the glory of God. Bravo! I thank all of you sincerely. May God richly bless you.

To my peers, mentors, grounders, and accountability partners, I appreciate each one of you. You have constantly kept me accountable and pressing on. For that, I am eternally grateful.

Special mention to Pastor Elijah Wanje (Senior Pastor, Ridgeways Baptist Church), Bishop Allan and Rev Kathy Kiuna (Church Founder and General Overseer, and Senior Associate Pastor respectively, Jubilee Christian Church), and Dr Kirimi Barine (Founder and Director, Publishing Institute of Africa): you all rock! I thank you for your guidance, mentorship, encouragement, prayers, and friendships. Most of all, I thank you for believing in me because it stirred up my gift. You have been my pillars of strength.

To my book project team, I thank each one of you for the part you played in making *Marriage Built to Last: Healing beyond Betrayal* a reality. Special mention to Pastor Fred Geke (Senior Pastor, Mercy Train Ministries), Rachel Wainaina-Walton (CEO, Anchored Families) and my editor, who wishes to remain in

Acknowledgements

the background: thank you most sincerely for your critique, valuable input, editorial work, and commitment to cheer me on to the finish line. For all that, I am truly grateful.

To my supportive children: daughters Rina, Ciru, and Chidi; and sons Kamau, Alan, and Bo, I could never have done this without your support and encouragement. Thank you for reading the manuscript and providing valuable feedback. I thank God for all of you.

To my husband Bob Karina, my number one fan and cheerleader: you motivate and inspire me. You urge me on always and hold me accountable. You are my rock, best friend, encourager, and confidant. Thank you for believing in and supporting me to achieve this dream, my second book. You have continued to pray over me for God to enlarge my territories, as I seek to empower God's people. Thank you for sponsoring this project.

Chapter One

A Nasty Surprise

In the early days, Anne could never stop talking about her marriage to John, a soft-spoken, focused, and hardworking man. A mutual friend had set them up after John's return from the United States of America, where he had studied and worked for close to twenty years. He wanted to resettle in Kenya and start a family. A gifted medical doctor, John spent the first two years planting his feet in a local medical practice. Once that was done, he began to look for someone to marry. Anne was suggested by friends and relatives.

When Anne and John first met, they did not seem like a match. While Anne is outspoken and forceful about what she wants in life, John says little and tends to accommodate the thoughts of other people. However, they had more things going for themselves. Anne had no time for men who did not know where they were headed; John knew where he wanted to go and even where he came from. He had a clear vision of the family he wanted and was a great manager of his work-life balance and finances. He needed a wife who could keep him organised and motivated, a role Anne fit perfectly.

They got married within a year of meeting. By the sixth month of their marriage, they had moved into their own house. Everything was going well except for a few challenges, which they dealt with. John worked long hours and so did Anne, an experienced accountant, but they tried to have at least one

Chapter One

meal together daily. They also arranged to spend a day each week to themselves. Life was good, until something happened to change all that.

One evening, Anne returned home to find the housemaid feeding a cute little boy. When she asked about the child, she was told that a lady had dropped him off "to be with his father". She called her husband immediately and demanded an explanation, after describing the scene. A shocked John explained that he could not do so that very moment; he had a patient. He assured her he would handle the situation and clarify things further, as soon as he arrived at the house.

Anne refused to listen. Was this John's child? Did he know about his son? How long ago? Who was the mother? Where was she? John tried to appease her, but she wanted her answers straightaway over the phone. Never a man of many words, all he could say was yes, the child was his from a past relationship. Anne called her mother-in-law next. John's mom was surprised Anne knew nothing about the boy. She assumed her son had told Anne about him during their courtship. By the time John got home that night, Anne was nowhere to be found. She had packed a bag and gone to her sister's house to make sense of everything.

John's story was simple. He had considered a return to Kenya five years earlier. As in Anne's case, another lady was introduced to him then. She had just joined university and he was smitten by her. John felt that she was "the one". Since he had only a couple of months off, he had had no time for a formal marriage. Instead, he had her move in with his parents, while he flew back to the States to arrange for her to join him. The girl dropped out of college to prepare for the relocation.

A Nasty Surprise

Two months later, she discovered she was pregnant. John received the news happily.

However, things started to fall apart. Because the girl's immigration papers were taking time to come together, new facts came to light during the wait. John's family found out about his fiancé's affair with a former boyfriend, funded by John's own money. His parents threw her out very quickly with his approval, but he still tried to stay in communication with her just to take care of and support the baby. Then the girl's own father and mother stepped in and told him to forget about the child just as he did their daughter. He had no choice but to cut off all ties with them. Until the girl took it upon herself to find him, John knew nothing of her and the baby's whereabouts all those intervening years. The first thing she did when she found John was to threaten him. She was going to leave the boy at his house. John did not take her seriously until Anne's frantic phone call.

As he drove home that night, in spite of the shocking development, John did not think anything could derail his marriage. He loved Anne. He believed that once he explained everything to her, she would understand and stand by him. When he did not find her at home, John realised the situation was graver than he had thought. He tried to phone her, but she refused to answer his calls. After about the tenth attempt, Anne's sister relented and spoke with him. She told him that Anne needed time alone before any discussion could take place. John remained optimistic that she would give him a chance to tell his story.

The opportunity never came. Anne spurned everyone's effort to iron out the couple's problem; she rebuffed John's brothers,

Chapter One

her friends, and even her own parents. She could never trust John again. In her mind, if he could lie or withhold information about that one thing, he could do the same for everything else. She wondered if she ever really knew John at all. Their once perfect marriage was hurtling towards a bitter divorce.

Self-Disclosure and the Value of Trust

It takes a lot to break a good marriage. John and Anne's was certainly a decent union, but it fell apart because what went wrong between them was the very thing one spouse could not handle. Sometimes, it is not the number of aberrations that counts but the degree and significance of each aberration and how a partner reacts to it. Clearly for Anne, trust is everything. When that was lost, nothing was left. A thousand good deeds could not make up for that one failure. A different wife might have seen John's nondisclosure as a small and solvable issue and would have dismissed Anne's reaction as over the top.

The lesson here is easy: No marriage is strong and stable enough not to be threatened by omissions or commissions. While they cannot be avoided altogether even in the best of marriages, such threats should be prevented whenever possible. Self-disclosure is one way to do so. It is the act of sharing about yourself to others, an essential part of building a healthy union.

Some people, however, feel they have legitimate reasons for not revealing their secrets. Sometimes, they are afraid of being judged and subsequently rejected. Often, they fear getting hurt or losing their newfound relationship. They might also think that what their loved ones do not know will not harm them anyway. Why introduce "unnecessary" information to a partner who is happy and settled? In John's case, he probably did not know how and when to bring it up. He may have assumed it unimportant because it was part of the past; it seemed to have no relevance to the present or his marriage's survival. In the end, whatever his reason, one thing is clear: John should have addressed the matter earlier. He owed the truth to Anne even before she had committed herself to him.

No doubt, sharing too many personal facts prematurely may threaten the other individual and the relationship. However, refusal to disclose vital information, especially involving children with an ex, may suggest deception, which risks the marriage even more. Since no confession is given at the beginning, the partner has no chance to decide whether to pursue the union or not. John may have feared losing Anne, but what he failed to realise was he ran a greater danger. By leaving her to stumble upon the details on her own, he deprived their relationship of intimacy and trust.

Suggested Steps in the Aftermath of Lost Trust

Work towards rebuilding your relationship even in the aftermath of lost trust. You have already given too much into it to let go without a fight. Walking away may seem the best option initially because of the pain you feel. However, if you shift your focus from the disappointment to your investment into the union, you may see matters differently.

Once one secret comes out, leave the doors open for all other secrets to be revealed. Talk about the issues in each disclosure. Say what needs to be said and listen to what you need to hear. Keep all channels of communication clear and unimpeded. While John's nondisclosure ignited a problem, the lack of a resolution is down to Anne's unwillingness to give him an opportunity to explain himself.

Inasmuch as your partner has hurt you, focus on what is important: the recovery of the relationship. Once issues have been dealt with, avoid talking about your pain further with friends and relatives. Reliving your disappointment will keep you stuck in the blues. Stay busy. Learn a new skill. Travel, if possible. Exercise positive thinking regardless of the challenges. Train yourself not to replay the problem. By all means, avoid throwing pity parties for yourself. Shun any extremes in both word and deed.

Do not revisit details of the disclosure with your spouse. Once you have talked it over and apologies have been exchanged and received, know that the worst has happened. Choose now to let go and ask yourself this question: if you were the offending party, how would you want your partner to treat you? That should keep you sober.

Often, the greatest victim in such circumstances is your self-esteem, so take steps to rebuild it. Give yourself and your personal brand a makeover. Make a conscious effort to look good. Read motivational and inspirational materials to lift up your spirits. If overwhelmed, seek the counsel of a therapist or a Christian minister, who will help you navigate the rough waters. As much as possible, leave your parents out of it. They may not know how to treat your partner even after you have resolved your issues.

Set ground rules and fresh boundaries with your spouse as you both move forward. Talk about your expectations of each other. Initially, have weekly meetings to evaluate your progress. Scale down the frequency of your meetings as time goes by.

You need time to heal from trust issues. Up to two years is a reasonable expectation, depending on the degree of betrayal. Be gentle on your partner and yourself. Do not have unrealistic hopes. Restore your connection with each other slowly by engaging in all levels of intimacy: emotional, intellectual, spiritual, physical, and recreational. Do not encourage a lengthy separation; it is not helpful.

If you are the offending party, do not try to justify your actions or minimise the effect they have on your partner. However, by the same measure, stop blaming yourself for them. Look towards rebuilding your relationship. If a third party is involved, avoid any further contact with that person; it can lead to a recurrence of the problem. You know the ill consequences of that.

Understand that resolving a serious marital issue does not guarantee a happily-ever-after. There is no such thing as a perfect marriage. There will always be issues to deal with: some serious, some innocuous; some expected, some out of the blue. For this reason, you as a couple need to take steps to eliminate those you can and prepare yourselves for the unexpected.

Moving Beyond the Resolution

The word "happy" is almost synonymous with marriage expectations; everyone hopes for a union made in heaven. However, after the romance, real issues must be confronted. The promise to love each other "for better or worse, in sickness and in health, until death do us part" gets severely tested throughout a marriage. Caught up in the excitement of wedding plans, many couples do not envision what their relationship will be like once everything settles down to a

Chapter One

routine. While Anne is justified in assuming trustworthiness from her partner, she probably stretched her hopes too far.

Anne is not alone in her situation. Many others find out about their spouses' children with other people before or already during the union. Either way, it hurts a lot. Above the pain, however, the more important things to concentrate on are your reaction and next steps. The shock revelation about John's son made Anne distrust him. As negative thoughts overwhelmed her, she chose to run away to her family. Had she wanted to redeem their marriage, Anne should have found a way to forgive John and to deal with their situation head on. Unfortunately, she focused on his untrustworthiness instead.

Many spouses harbour doubts about their partners not because they have no faith in them or do not love them enough; they are simply afraid of the unknown. Did I make the right decision? Will the relationship work? Their doubts are neither strange nor unusual, but they can become a problem when individuals fail to move beyond the fear and enjoy the union.

While aspiring for a "perfect" marriage may be a pipe dream, here are some pointers to establish and celebrate a good one:

Know yourself. Develop self-awareness. How do you react to situations? What is your love language? In other words, what actions communicate love to you? What conveys the opposite? If you know the answers to these questions, you might be able to understand your own desires, fears, expectations, and even fantasies.

Take responsibility. Own up to your part of the problem. While John is guilty of withholding vital information about his past, Anne is also guilty of an unreasonably hard stance. Until she found out about the child, she was a hundred percent behind her husband's integrity and reliability as a friend, lover, and provider. She may need to admit to previous issues in her life that had nothing to do with John.

Communicate. No marriage foundation or restoration can be complete without avenues of and skills in communication. If you and your partner can express your thoughts and feelings, you can resolve conflicts better. When it is impossible to do so without sparking an argument, ironing out problems becomes impossible. Discuss first what you need to feel safe and comfortable before sharing anything. For many couples, a specific time or place to talk about important matters might spell the difference. The following pointers from experts can go a long way in improving your communication with each other:

1. **Use positive language.** Make every effort to adopt an encouraging tone during your conversations, so they do not become heated arguments but opportunities to grow. Being overly critical may cost you chances to nurture and be supportive.
2. **Be aware of your body language.** It represents over eighty percent of communication. Ensure that it matches your words; consistency is crucial at all times. Maintain good eye contact as it is powerful and conveys interest. It encourages your partner to engage at a deeper and more meaningful level.
3. **Manifest constructive attitudes and beliefs**. They have a huge impact on the way you compose yourself and interact with your partner. Be sensitive, respectful, and honourable always. When you separate your feelings from the actual circumstances and events on hand, you help

your partner feel less defensive and more willing to listen. A gentle answer turns away wrath, but a harsh word stirs up anger.

4. **Develop active listening skills.** They are designed to make it easier to converse about sensitive issues and to deepen your understanding and appreciation of your partner. When practicing it, the speaker must remain focused on a single point. On the other hand, the listener must concentrate on the other's perspective while discovering new insights about the spouse's own thoughts and feelings. No matter what the topic is, the most important part of active listening is to do it with patience and love.

5. **Grow closer.** People change over time, often in surprising or unexpected ways. Being in a long-term relationship can make it easy to overlook new aspects of your partner's personal growth, temperaments, and personality. You will have trouble communicating, if you cannot easily accept the changes. Even the most well-meaning efforts can fail if you are unable to relate to your spouse's interests and passions.

6. **Spend quality time together.** Maintaining a relationship requires hard work, so it is important for you as a couple to relax and unwind. Arrange a trip or time away together to bond and have fun. Following the same routine or staying in the same surroundings can cause a relationship to stagnate. Being together in a new environment can allow you both to create fresh memories while alleviating the stress that makes communication difficult.

Reflection

Get rid of all bitterness, rage and anger, brawling, and slander, along with every form of malice. Be kind and compassionate to one another, forgiving each other, just as in Christ God forgave you. (Ephesians 4:31-32)

Chapter Two

In the Shadow of the Ex

Mike's world came tumbling down a few months ago when he discovered his wife of three years regularly communicating with her ex-boyfriend. They sometimes even met for a cup of coffee. Anita did not deny having contact with her ex. She believed her husband was overreacting and the real problem was his insecurity. Mike did not think so. From the beginning of their relationship, Ben had always been a shadow they could not shake off.

Before their courtship and eventual marriage, Mike and Anita were colleagues at an insurance firm. At that time, Anita was engaged to her high-school sweetheart—or so she thought. She had known Ben since she was fourteen. In time, their teenage friendship evolved into a deep relationship that everybody assumed would end in marriage. Both knew each other's families and friends.

They kept the flame burning through college and their early working days. However, trouble broke out in paradise in 2009, when Ben started to become aloof. His calls came less frequently and, when they did come, they were cold and unproductive. Their dates were even worse. Usually an animated conversationalist, Ben suddenly had nothing to say and was strangely irritable, especially when pressed to explain his behaviour. At first, he denied any problem. When he eventually opened up, it knocked Anita out cold.

Chapter Two

Ben explained that he did not love her and felt trapped in a childhood commitment that could not be sustained by adult realities. He had stayed in the relationship for two reasons. First, he did not want to hurt Anita; second, he did not intend to disappoint their families and friends who believed their marriage a foregone conclusion. He was tired of living a lie and decided to call it quits.

Nothing could have prepared Anita for that. She was devastated and her life became a haze. She cried often and hardly ate anything. She could not open up to her loved ones, so she suffered quietly. The first person to notice something was amiss was her colleague, Mike, because they shared a workstation. Although initially reluctant to talk, Anita eventually opened up to him. He gave her a shoulder to cry on. Whenever the intense pain threatened to crush her heart at night, she would phone and wake him up. While she bared her heart to him, he did his best to listen and be a friend. In time, Anita began to look forward to their chats, occasional lunches, or coffee. It did not take long before her heart began to fall for him. Although her feelings towards Ben never diminished, she found a new possibility in Mike.

For Mike, things were a bit more complicated. He was twelve years older than Anita was and a senior bachelor. Marriage had never been a priority in his life. He was not the romantic type. Expressions like "I love you" and "I miss you" did not come naturally to him. However, what he lacked in ardour, he made up for in pragmatism and reliability. He kept his word and provided faithfully. While he did not give flowers to Anita, he did go out to buy the largest and most convenient fridge for her.

In the Shadow of the Ex

Two years after Anita fell into Mike's arms, they got married. She seemed to have come to terms with her previous loss and took up her new role as wife, with zest. Mike was caring and supportive, and treated her like a fragile pet, sometimes bordering on overprotectiveness. By this time, Anita's feelings towards Ben had come full circle. Love had turned into pain and disappointment, then anger, then hate and resentment, and then finally, back to love and longing. With her marriage, the memory of her ex was pushed deep into the recesses of her mind.

All that changed one evening when she ran into Ben at a supermarket queue, when she felt a light tap on her shoulder. She turned and saw Ben standing in front of her. "Hi, Annie. Beautiful as always."

Anita did not know what to feel or say. They shared small, awkward talk and said goodbye when they reached the cashier. As Anita walked towards her car, a part of her was happy to see him. The rest was seething with anger. She did not mention the incident to Mike but could not get it out of her mind. A few weeks later, she received a Facebook friend request from Ben. The same mix of emotions overwhelmed her, so she ignored it. A month later, Ben sent her a Facebook message:

"I understand your shutting me out. I would have done the same in your shoes. Just wanted to say that I had no right to treat you as I did. Your husband is a lucky man because we both know you are a great woman. Best wishes. Forgive my intrusion."

Beside herself with anger, she began furiously to type a reply. "Great woman indeed! Do great women get dumped by the roadside after ten years?" She could not get herself to hit the send button. Instead, she found herself crying. Once she had composed herself, she deleted her original message and wrote instead, "When did you find out I'm a great woman?"

The following day, she received a lengthy, very apologetic reply from Ben, who explained the genesis of his "confusion". He detailed where his life had gone from their breakup and the mess he had gotten himself into. He signed off by emphasising his respect for her marriage. He believed he deserved the disappointment his life was now.

From then on, the daily exchange never stopped. Anita was anxious to know what had happened and he was eager to explain. All that called for time on Facebook. Along the way, Mike noticed his wife suddenly spending a lot of time online. Alarmed, he confronted her. After some time of denial, Anita admitted to communicating with her ex. Mike could not believe what she said, knowing what Ben had done to her. Worse, she even appeared to defend him. On her part, Anita believed she was just being a friend to someone who had made a mistake and was paying the price. She asserted that Mike was too valuable to her; she could not contemplate leaving him. She insisted that Ben's previous ill treatment of her was not enough reason to abandon him totally, as they had a long history together.

Untangling the Intricacies of the Issue

It is not strange to desire what you once had and held close to your heart. However, things begin to go wrong when you start to entertain the thought of reaching out to someone who is already in another committed relationship. Inasmuch as Anita believes her actions are harmless and noble, she endangers herself. By holding on to her feelings for Ben, she exposes herself to temptation and she delays her ability to connect and grow in intimacy with Mike.

Feelings of love for an ex can continue for any number of reasons. Your life is an accumulation of loves and losses. Sometimes, you decide who you date based on lessons learned from failed relationships. Your collection of love experiences represents and validates the breadth of your loving self.

You may have gone through a breakup but continue to think of and fantasise about your ex, even though you now have a new relationship. You would think, after marrying your 'prince charming,' that there is no one else you would want in life! Happily-ever-after becomes your portion. You have neither need nor reason for any other person, especially your ex! So why do you still desire someone besides your spouse?

Sometimes, the shared bonds of emotional and physical intimacies with an ex cannot be easily broken. Still, your ex should remain that: an ex—someone who once was but now is not. Under no circumstances should you retain items such as photographs, gifts, or love letters from that relationship. They have a way of awakening emotions and triggering a romance. You should avoid constant communication. Don't give your spouse a reason to be jealous of a previous romance.

People say, "I am really enjoying a relationship with my ex-lover. I know it's wrong, but it's the best thing that has ever happened to me. I have a problematic marriage. After a long time, I have found happiness and fulfilling sex again. Everything is magical! I know this could be the beginning of the end of my marriage. I cannot bear to lose my husband or to have my children without their father, but I cannot help myself." And this is why exes must be avoided at all costs.

Chapter Two

It is easy to fall back and rekindle a relationship that can break up a marriage and family, so make a conscious decision to stay away from your ex. Give yourself the opportunity to build an intimate relationship with your spouse instead. Setting deliberate boundaries early in the new bond is vital. Here are some tips to help you deal with a former lover and to avoid suffocating your present relationship:

Make a commitment and respect it. If two people are not committed to each other, their marriage will fall apart sooner or later. Trust is the foundation of a good marriage and it begins with unfaltering commitment. Your partner needs to know that you are promising yourself to him and to your marriage together, regardless of any challenges. Your vow must include a willingness to break away from the past, so you can build a future together. Your ex should be part of that past.

The traditional marriage vow states, "For better or worse, for richer or poorer, in sickness and in health, to love, to honour, and to cherish, until death do us part." Commitment looks beyond the present into a future that you plan for and enter together as partners. Today may crowd you with seemingly insurmountable problems, but the truth is that they are part of life.

Your commitment should include planning together because, without a joint vision, you cannot set a goal or direction. You can wander around in circles or slip into a dreaded downward spiral. Dreams give you clarity, energy, motivation, and hope. Do not get stuck in the present and its baggage from the past. Aspire for a big future.

Be content. When you hear the word "contentment", you think of money and material possessions. However, contentment extends into many other areas of life, including marriage. Marriage is among the most important areas in which you must seek and find satisfaction.

To be content is to be mentally and emotionally satisfied with the way things are. If you are fulfilled, you can accept current, though imperfect, circumstances with peace of mind. If you are discontented with your marriage, you make yourself and your spouse miserable. You are never satisfied with what you have. You always want, expect, or even demand more. Instead of recognising the positive aspects of your spouse and marriage, you focus on the negatives. Instead of appreciation and encouragement, you express criticism and resentment.

Obviously, Anita was not content in her marriage, so it was easy for her to be swayed by her ex. It is helpful to deal with an ex's loss, ideally with an expert, before engaging in another relationship that leads to marriage. Have closure first and deal with all the pain, anger, resentment, and frustration. Say what needs to be said. After all that, move on.

You do not need a perfect marriage to be content, but you must have a positive attitude and outlook, if you want to find contentment. Begin by counting your blessings; do not take them for granted. Marital problems are best approached from a position of general contentment rather than from that of perpetual displeasure or misery. People respond best to positive reinforcement and encouragement; your spouse is no different. In life and in marriage, contentment is a virtue; exercise it.

Create new boundaries. Keep your ex at a distance. No phone calls, emails, and texting. And definitely no late-night visits. You should steer clear of your ex by all means. But what if you cannot completely cut off contact because you have children together, run a business jointly, or belong to the same company? Your recovery will be little bit more challenging but not impossible. You just have to create special limits, dealing with your ex only when absolutely necessary and strictly about your common interests: the kids, the enterprise, or work.

And what if your ex wants to know how you are handling the breakup? Avoid details because they provide an opportunity for an emotional connection. Do not pry into your ex's post-breakup situation either. Just as you deserve to heal and move on, so does your ex. Give your ex the space and time to do so.

A word of caution: when you feel disappointment, do not seek comfort in the arms of your ex. It is dangerous because of your familiarity with each other. Instead, recruit a support system from your inner circle of friends, preferably those who have your best interests at heart and will not report back to your ex on your progress and setbacks. This is one of the single, most important steps you can follow during your recovery.

It is possible to have a platonic relationship with an ex. However, you must redefine the relationship. For your spouse's and your comfort, keep ex-lovers at a distance in the relationship because they could cost you your marriage.

Are You in a Rebound Relationship?

You might be one of those people who think a relationship that happens after a breakup or during a rough time in your life is what will bring you fulfilment, contentment, and happiness. However, it does not always do that. Instead, it can bring about anxiety, disappointment, and regret. One woman shared:

"My boyfriend and I started to experience major conflict for no apparent reason. There always seemed to be a reason to fight. Simple misunderstandings turned into serious conflicts. We couldn't see eye to eye on anything anymore. The harder I tried, the worse it got. We agreed to take some time off to cool things down. But before I knew it, I had already hooked up with an old friend and we do so well together. It's perfect! Now and then though, I find myself confused. I still miss my boyfriend, but I do enjoy this new man in my life."

Generally, when you break up with someone and then immediately get into a new relationship with another person, you are trying to prove yourself worthy of love and affection. Perhaps you desire and miss the triple-A dose: affection, attention, and affirmation. To feed your ego and boost your self-esteem, you extract it from the new bond. You feed your personal worth and enjoy it greatly.

It is important to be true to yourself and test whether your motives are sincere. If the breakup had not happened, would you be in a relationship with the new person or are you simply feeding your ego and living in denial? Have you taken time to reflect on and resolve the conflict with your previous partner? Have you explored all options for reconciliation?

You have to remember that the need to mask pain can drive you into more agony, which is the biggest problem in a rebound. Usually, someone ends up being used and hurt. Guess what? It could be you. If you are in a relationship to distract yourself from the pain of a breakup, do yourself a favour and step aside. Acknowledge your emotions and seek healing before getting into another romantic relationship.

A shoulder to cry on is necessary, so it is easy for you to mistake the new relationship for romance and to fantasise about it to suit your immediate needs: love and a sense of belonging. This state is only temporary. You may simply be enjoying the fresh personality and deliberately closing your eyes to his flaws. Whatever the case may be, wake up and save yourself the disappointment and pain.

On the other hand, you may be spending a significant amount of time focusing on your previous partner, wondering what went wrong, and considering a second round. When you concentrate on your ex and everything related to him, you sabotage the success of your new relationship, so sort out what you need to do first before moving on. Do not engage in another relationship immediately after a breakup. Take time to heal.

The Four Stages of Marriage

Marriage goes through four defined stages: dream, drama, discovery, and depth. After the dream stage, it is not uncommon for partners to reach out to past lovers, searching for the now-fleeting, feel-good factor and fantasy. Sometimes, there is so much conflict drama that an ex-lover can come in handy to fill the void.

I often come across individuals who feel that they had made a mistake in marrying their partner. They are bored and believe that they would be happier if they had married one of their exes instead. Some experience a relationship shift a few months into their marriage. What they go through is normal; they do not understand it is just a stage. Recognise the stage and season you are in.

Dream Stage

This stage is so good; you wish it would last forever, although it normally may last for the first two years. Your heart is filled with love and passion. It is sometimes referred to as the stage of "loving under the influence" because, according to Hendrix, the brain is flooded with feel-good neurochemicals such as dopamine and phenylethylamine. Their effect on behaviour is the same as that of endorphin. Endorphin increases energy, feelings of well-being, a positive outlook, and sexual desire.

During this period, the relationship is characterised by deep romance. It matches our fantasies about marriage. Sexual attraction and the desire to be together and share everything are strong. It is common to believe that your partner makes you shine, brings out the best in you. Sometimes, partners develop codependency at this stage, which may eventually pose a challenge to the relationship. For most people, this stage simply does not last long enough. If you are still in this stage right now, enjoy it! But remember: it will last for only a season.

In time, energies devoted to sex lessen to make way for other responsibilities. When it happens, you may wrongly assume that something has gone wrong; your relationship no longer works. You think you may no longer be in love with your partner because you do not feel the fire anymore. You may no longer feel attracted to each other as you did at the beginning. No need to panic; simply acknowledge that your relationship is maturing and you are ready to move to the next level.

Chapter Two

Drama Stage

This stage is characterised by disappointment, distress, power struggles, loneliness, regret, and other similar feelings associated with settling down. Hendrix explains that the decline of neurochemicals becomes evident and results in low sexual energies. Sex may become routine and not as spontaneous and enjoyable as it once was. Children—already born or expected—require increased responsibilities on your part and can give rise to all manner of reactions. Because of the challenges of this stage, it is common for partners to reach out to past lovers, which opens the door to infidelity.

At this stage, you may be ready to throw in the towel. You may think there is nothing left in your union. You and your spouse do not agree on anything and constantly fight about everything, even though you believed, like most couples entering marriage, you will never fight because you love each other. Despair, disappointment, and hopelessness set in. Many couples I have interacted with at this stage claim "this is not the person I married" and that they choose to stay together only because of the children.

The truth is, any two people placed together for whatever reason will experience conflict at one time or another just because they are different from each other. However, finding a new partner or going back to a previous one is not the solution here. Instead, use your difficulties as learning experiences. They can unlock opportunities for intimacy and fulfilment in your relationship.

At a seminar on relationships and fidelity, many participants were shocked to discover how attached they still were to their past lovers. Some admitted receiving phone calls from them on a regular basis and exchanging messages on various social media. They loved to know that their former lovers still thought of them. They were thrilled to experience the tingling sensation running up and down their spine again! Exciting, yes, but very dangerous to a marriage. Do not to allow yourself to remain in this stage too long. Do not let the confusion and stress overwhelm you and draw you away from your spouse. Have a good communication. Be open and compassionate with each other.

Discovery and Depth Stages

You can make it through the previous stage by nurturing communication and allowing vulnerability, honesty, and trust to be your foundation. For most couples, the discovery phase does not happen until after their tenth year of marriage. It is a comfortable place but still has its challenges.

You may find and create a new sense of connection. You both learn more about each other's strengths and weaknesses. You also become skilled at identifying and talking about your fears instead of acting them out. You no longer judge or blame your partner. Instead, you translate his complaint into requests for change. You stop being critical. You work on winning strategies to move the relationship forward despite the difficulties. You complement one another and accommodate each other's shortcomings without effort.

The downside of this stage is that there is not so much spark in your love life or conflict anymore. You both turn your attention outward, focusing on your children, work, and friendships. If you do not observe balance, you drift into your comfort zones. Before you know it, you live separate lives as if you were single.

Chapter Two

In his frustration, David had this to say: "Since my wife began to pursue her college education, she is either at school, catching up with her study partner, or somewhere else, working on her assignments. She sleeps late. To her, I do not seem to exist. She is always preoccupied with her books and has no time even for the children. I feel neglected, lonely, and concerned. We do not have quality time anymore."

You might also identify with David's dilemma. You and your partner must structure your time together. It is easy for careers, education, and children to eclipse a marriage. Remember that jobs and children will not always be there, but your spouse will be until death do you part. Do yourself a favour and navigate this stage with wisdom. It is rewarding when you do so effectively. You view one another in a new light, with increased empathy and compassion. You discover ways to appreciate and respect each other and not take one another for granted.

It is exciting and fulfilling when you and your partner find a balance and grow towards oneness as you enhance your intimacy levels, both individually and collectively. Your thinking becomes more expansive and inclusive. You experience renewed energies as you focus on gratitude and thanksgiving.

Failure to accomplish the tasks of one stage can inhibit movement and growth through later stages. Compromise, commitment, and dedication help move your relationship to the final level of depth, where you can enjoy a deeply rooted bond.

The Soul-Tie Syndrome

Here is a story I often hear: "I am married but cannot get over my ex. I want to be happy and enjoy my marriage, but I suffer from guilt because I'm still in love with the other person. It affects my relationship in a terrible way." If that sounds like your story, please note: you are experiencing a soul-tie syndrome.

A soul tie is the knitting together of two individual souls emotionally, physically, and spiritually. There are good and bad soul ties. Good soul ties are commonly created in marriage and healthy friendships. They can bring tremendous blessings to you. Bad soul ties happen in wrong, illicit, or sinful connections and can cause tremendous destruction.

One way a soul tie is formed is through sexual relationships. A marriage is said to be consummated only after sex. Consummation is a legal term that characterises the fulfilment of a marriage. Its absence can nullify a marital union. If you were an unmarried person, every single time you have sex with someone, you let that person leave a part of himself in you and vice versa. Sex outside marriage rips and tears the soul when you try to break away. Remember that it joins you together as one, so when you try to part ways, it hurts you, leaving behind emotional scars that affect your future relationships.

Words play a great role in establishing soul ties. When you each make vows like "I will love you forever", "I will never leave you", "You are the only one I will ever love", or "I got your back no matter what", you tend to hold on to those words even when you move on. You hold on to that commitment, denying yourself the privilege of enjoying your current relationship.

How do you break away?

Be aware because awareness is the heartbeat of therapy. Acknowledge your unhealthy past. Avoid the person and ask God to give you the strength to move on.

Chapter Two

Get rid of gifts given to you by your ex. Any gifts of any kind from your former partner (ex) should be returned, given away, or destroyed. If you are still friends or in an unhealthy relationship, accept that it is in your best interest to walk away.

Renounce any vows or commitments made. The tongue has the ability to bring the soul great troubles and bondage. Spoken vows can follow you throughout your life and need to be broken.

Admit the pain and begin a journey of healing. If the soul tie came about from physical or sexual abuse, you should recognise the ache, let go of the past, and throw away the baggage. Ask God to give you the courage, strength, and ability to move on.

Seek God's wisdom to find a mentor, pastor, or coach to help you explore matters if you are stuck and need help to move on. Your life is precious. Live, love, and thrive because you deserve it.

Reflection

Therefore, I urge you, brothers and sisters, in view of God's mercy, to offer your bodies as a living sacrifice, holy and pleasing to God—this is your true and proper worship. Do not conform to the pattern of this world, but be transformed by the renewing of your mind. Then you will be able to test and approve what God's will is—his good, pleasing, and perfect will. For by the grace given me I say to every one of you: Do not think of yourself more highly than you ought, but rather think of yourself with sober judgment, in accordance with the faith God has distributed to each of you. (Romans 12:1-3)

Chapter Three

Impossible to Please

"I should have seen it coming, but I didn't," Sherry admitted. "The signs were there from our early days, but not once did I realise that it would come to this."

Sherry was talking about her husband's low self-esteem. When they first met, all she saw was a young, successful businessman, always on the go to get to the next deal. She noticed Jeff's particular attention to everything, especially his clothes and the manner he wore them, but nobody complained about such a smart, neat man. He had his accomplishments to show for it. Sometimes, Sherry got uncomfortable whenever they went out to eat and he would complain about the waiters, but she forgave him his obsession with details.

When they began to date, a new side of Jeff emerged. He would phone her several times a day to ask how she was doing. Sherry had never received so much attention in her life; she found it flattering and revelled in it. Sometimes, he would drop by her workplace unexpectedly, with a packed lunch or a midmorning snack. As their relationship progressed, however, Sherry realised that all the calls and surprise visits were not actions of a caring man; he was trying to keep tabs on her. Jeff went to her office to let everyone know that she was taken. Still, she did not think it a problem. Was it unreasonable for anyone to be possessive over someone they loved deeply? She responded by doing everything to reassure him of her commitment.

Chapter Three

As their relationship deepened, he became more controlling. Whenever she received a call, he wanted to know the caller. If it was a man, he would cross-examine her about their relationship and then give her a lengthy lecture about the untrustworthiness of other men. He warned her to stay away from them completely. Again, it all sounded fair to Sherry, although she could have done without Jeff's talk-down. She bent over backwards and let go of a few male friends. She adjusted her life to accommodate his concerns and fears.

As time wore on, however, it became very clear that for every issue Sherry dealt with, two others took its place. Soon, she started to dread her dates with Jeff. If anyone greeted her, she had to explain who it was to him. The whole scenario began to take a toll on her. While she appreciated Jeff's love, she felt hemmed in. One evening, it all blew up in her face.

They were having dinner when Jeff suggested they should share their email and Facebook passwords. He thought it fair, since they were a couple. While Sherry had nothing to hide, she felt strongly against it and said so. Jeff flew off the handle and accused her of seeing other men behind his back. She countered his accusations, but he kept insisting that only people with dark secrets would refuse to give up their passwords. Their fight was so bad that night; Sherry decided to call it quits.

The following morning, when she arrived at work, Sherry found an email from Jeff waiting for her. In it, he continued his allegations, including that she slept with her boss. He reminded her about the money that he had spent on her for gifts and holidays and challenged her to name any other of her "men" who could afford to give her that lifestyle. Sherry did not reply to his letter. Several more followed over the next week, but she trashed them quickly without reading. She was ready to move on with her life.

Weeks into the breakup, Sherry began to wonder if she had done the right thing. While she was still upset with Jeff's behaviour, she also missed him. As she wrestled with her emotions, his next email came. This time, she opened it. The message was a long one filled with profuse apologies and deep regrets. Jeff admitted he had a problem and needed help. He described Sherry as the only woman who had ever understood him. Could she forgive him and grant him a chance to begin again with her?

They had tea and a long talk soon afterwards. Jeff was subdued and eager to agree with everything she said. He apologised repeatedly and promised never to behave that way with her again. That evening, he brought out an expensive ring and proposed to her. Sherry said yes and they got married immediately. They both felt marriage provided the necessary assurances to protect their relationship from petty jealousies. And for a while, it did. Then the old Jeff resurfaced; this time, he was many times worse.

Jeff criticised everything Sherry did and reminded her how lucky she was to be married to him. He accused her family of being proud. He then began to control every aspect of her life, demanding her job resignation to stay at home. He reasoned that they did not need the money. Because she wanted the marriage to work, Sherry yielded to his insistence. But sadly, nothing she did satisfied him anyway. The more she gave in to his domination, the more he came up with new ways to manipulate her. The more she met his standards, the more he found things to disparage about her. The more she tried to please him, the more worthless he made her feel. "In his eyes, I could do no right," Sherry recalled. "I felt worthless. I blamed myself for not being good enough for my successful husband."

A year into their marriage, Sherry could no longer tolerate it. One day, while Jeff was out of the house, she packed her bags and left. As before, he called and belittled her inability to live without him. He reminded her that he had money to hire the best divorce lawyer to reduce her to nothing. When bullying did not work, Jeff fell back on copious apologies and promises. Only when he suggested marital counselling did Sherry agree to give their marriage another try. It was during their sessions that Jeff's low self-esteem issues came up.

Some Costs of Self-Esteem and Self-Worth Issues

Almost everyone faces self-esteem issues at one time or another in their life journey. For some, the battles surface in their adolescence; for others, they show up in their young adult or mature years. As in Jeff's case, some struggles manifest in relationships or social interactions; others, in careers, making them feel incompetent or inadequately skilled to perform their jobs. Often, the internal strife can be a long-term experience, but many burdened with low self-esteem may not even recognise it. Certainly, they may not realise how much their actions and reactions hurt those around them. They perform about their daily activities, hoping nobody sees their inner conflicts. What they do not understand is that their low self-esteem not only hurts them but also destroys their love relationships and, consequently, themselves.

People's experiences greatly influence their self-esteem and personal development. Positive or negative life events may create attitudes towards the self, which can be favourable and develop affirmative feelings of self-worth or unfavourable and lead to adverse ones. The resultant emotions can affect these individuals' relationships with their significant others. According to Rosenberg and Owen, people with low self-esteem are more troubled by failure and tend to interpret events as mostly being bad, even when they are not.

Your attitude and self-image determine if you will find happiness and fulfilment. Before you can find contentment from others, you must first be content with yourself. Your attitude is often determined by your level of self-worth, which is your estimation of who you are. If it is positive, you become confident in yourself, but if you have a low self-esteem, the effects will not be good for either of you in your relationship. You often become too wrapped up in your own anxieties to be open to and available for your partner. As an example: Jeff's insecurities made him belligerent, jealous, and close-minded towards Sherry, effectively pushing her away. In turn, his attitude towards her made her feel alone in the marriage and inadequate. "In his eyes, I could do no right," she observed. "I felt worthless. I blamed myself for not being good enough for my successful husband."

As Jeff continued his attacks on Sherry, even their sex life became adversely affected. This is because great sex happens only when two whole people surrender to each other and connect at an intimate and passionate level. To enjoy coitus, the mind needs to be free from any inhibitions. Preoccupations with being "good enough" bring tension and poor performance;

criticisms make it worse. How can I sleep with someone who rejects me and does not care for me at all? In such a scenario, "not tonight" becomes the standard response. Because you are always worried about what your spouse thinks of you, you cannot really be present in the bedroom. Sex is always fun, but when you are not bonding, it is not making love. And when it is not that, sex eventually becomes bland, boring, and stale.

Addressing Self-Esteem and Self-Worth Issues

Here is the good news: low self-esteem can be reversed. There are ways to help you, so you can be free to enter into and enjoy relationships. Although your low self-esteem hurts you and others, you can control it. Actually, you are the only one who can do something about it. Tackling your low self-esteem is a release that helps you feel better about yourself and enables your partner to be more in love with you. Read inspiring books on self-esteem. Seek the services of a professional counsellor, if necessary, and embark on a journey of personal development. It will be worth your while.

Resist putting yourself down. Be gentle with yourself, when you fail. If you have been undervaluing yourself for a long time, a kind attitude towards yourself may not come easily. It does not mean you cannot do it. You can learn to appreciate yourself. You have no choice but to work on your self-esteem, so you can realise your true worth and experience your partner's love and respect. You have to bring yourself to where you believe it is right and prudent for others to love you and to be positive towards you.

A partner who criticises you at every opportunity harms your self-esteem, as in Sherry's case. However, in every relationship, there is a place for positive criticism. It provides opportunities for you and the other person to improve and to grow. Criticism from others or yourself is a feedback mechanism to help you improve your personal bonds. When the criticism becomes repetitive and is delivered in an insensitive and demeaning manner, it does not achieve its intended purpose. Strive to take a different approach. Positive criticism should clearly identify the problem and suggest interventions for it. Criticism without a way forward is negative. Endeavour to give healthy suggestions as to how your partner could improve. In this way, you can promote problem-solving while helping him attain the desired behaviour.

Jeff and Sherry's relationship would not have reached the stage it did had they sought help much earlier. If your partner continues to be critical, then try to address the question: "What is behind this criticism?" When a partner is being judgemental, as Jeff was, the issue may be something else. His nitpicking was an expression of his own inadequacies and/or insecurities.

A Focus on Positive Criticism

It is not uncommon for a partner to take criticism too personally and to react emotionally than to face facts. Women are particularly guilty because we are naturally emotional. Feelings play a major role in how relational we choose to be. The reaction may be unreasonable and, at times, takes the criticism out of context. It misses out on given facts and becomes illogical. Always listen with a commitment to make sense of what your partner is trying to communicate.

Stay on the issue at hand and avoid bringing up other issues unrelated to the current situation. As much as possible, provide an appraisal that is fact-centred and about the present, not the past. Blaming is usually at the core of poorly expressed criticism and forces your partner to take a defensive position. Avoid using blame when stating a need to your partner. Say, "Let's have dinner together this Friday because I love being with you," not "You should take me out to dinner this Friday because you are never available on other days." Similarly, "I enjoy every moment we spend together" is more effective than "You never have time for me".

If you are an overly critical partner, you can damage your spouse's self-worth and self-esteem. Hurtful words have the potential to wound individuals for life and affect their capacity to connect intimately. If your partner puts you down and never affirms you but always points out something negative about you—too fat, too short, useless, good for nothing—making you feel worthless, it is time to say no to the criticism. Do not let it ruin your life or your relationship.

Excessive criticism is not a normal part of a relationship and should not be tolerated. It is important not to blame yourself. Do not take responsibility for the offender's actions. No one is perfect; we all have faults. Do not take the criticism personally; deal with the issues constructively. Regardless of the surrounding circumstances, do not let your partner's critical behaviour go unquestioned. Do not give up expressing yourself. Do not become tired and weary of defending yourself. Stand up!

Fear of conflict causes partners to avoid a discussion of their feelings. They become afraid of damaging the relationship. This can be dangerous as hurt feelings can go unattended and ignored. If disregarded, it can fester and turn into resentment and retaliation. On the other hand, a criticised partner can also take a defensive stand and become aggressive or very combative.

Has your self-worth been affected by your partner's negative actions? The following questions can help you find out:

1. Do you need somebody else to acknowledge your worth, so you can recognise and believe it yourself?
2. Do you crave outside affirmation of your value most of the time?
3. Do you easily accept compliments?
4. Do you always criticise and put yourself down?
5. Do you feel insecure?
6. Do you focus on your weaknesses and the injustices done to you?
7. Do you constantly make excuses for the abuse you experience?

If your answer is yes to most of the above questions, then you need to work on your self-worth.

How to Deal with a Partner's Negative Criticism

First, understand that negative criticism is emotional abuse. Make every effort to counter the adverse messages of your partner. Practice assertive skills and address the disparagement as soon as ideal, before it becomes a habit. At the opportune time, repeat to him what he said to you and let him know how you felt. Discuss the issues openly with him. Tell him to stop using hurtful words. On the other hand, you also need to let go of the pain from the things he may have said. Seek professional help when things get out of hand. Denial cannot heal you.

You must take action before you lose yourself in the shadows. Remember always that you are valuable. Make every effort to live, love, and thrive because you deserve it.

What you think and speak about yourself is very crucial. Be your own best encourager and speak positively about yourself. Spend time with people who value you, who affirm and encourage you, and who bring out the best in you. Be patient with yourself and with others. Nobody is perfect! When you make a mistake, accept it and work your way towards restoration.

When you have low self-esteem, you can become depressed. You can also become tolerant of abusive situations and relationships, which is harmful to you in many ways. On the other hand, if you have an exaggerated self-esteem, you can have an undeserved feeling of entitlement and an inability to learn from failures. Strive to maintain a balance and be sensitive to yourself and to those around you.

Reflection

5 "Before I formed you in the womb I knew [a] you,
before you were born I set you apart;
I appointed you as a prophet to the nations."
(Jeremiah 1:5)

11 "For I know the plans I have for you, 'Declare The Lord,' plans to prosper you and not to harm you, plans to give you hope and a future."- (Jeremiah 29:11)

Chapter Four

Hidden Wealth

Grace still remembers her school days. Because of the challenges she faced then, she has done everything in her power to become the woman she is today. She has no plans of getting married, even though she is already in her late thirties. Grace believes she has good reason for shunning marriage.

Her late father was a civil servant. He stayed by himself wherever his job took him, but Grace's mother lived with the children in their village. Although her father held a fairly senior position in government, there was never enough money to provide a decent life for Grace and her five siblings. Throughout primary school, they attended classes barefoot. Whenever they were sent home for unpaid school fees, their mother would have to scrounge around by herself to put together something to facilitate their return to school. Meantime, their father would come home whenever it suited him. Even when he was with them, he never did anything to alleviate the family's financial struggles. He would always talk about having no money. On occasion, he would even sell off one of the family animals, saying he had urgent monetary needs to meet.

At age thirteen, Grace joined high school. Her mother did what she could to buy her required items for her. Her father sent part of her fees but explained that the rest would have to come in the course of the month. Set up in such a situation,

Chapter Four

Grace had a very challenging time ahead of her. Although she remained competitive academically, she was constantly reminded of her disadvantaged social status. She participated in sports without any shoes because she had none for such activities. She could not afford sugar or any beverage to make herself a drink at night as the other girls did. She was the butt of many jokes, often being tagged "the villager". Her worst tormentor was a girl named Nancy.

Nancy's family was well-to-do. She had all the money and supplies a schoolgirl could ask for and did not waste time in flaunting her privilege. And because her mother and brother visited her often, she was always able to replenish her provisions with comforts from home. On the other hand, no one ever visited Grace until she graduated. Many times, she was sent back to the village for fees, sometimes staying there for several weeks while waiting for her father to do something. Occasionally, he ignored her situation altogether, so her mother had to go on a begging mission among her siblings. They would help but wondered why their brother-in-law could not support his own children. The answer did not come until Grace finished high school and prepared to join university. Thankfully, she had done quite well and looked forward to securing a university loan to pay for her studies. Nancy had not done as well as Grace had.

Around that time, Grace's father lost his job and there was even talk of a case against him over missing government funds. He came home and relearned the ropes of village life. Grace's mother did not hide her resentment towards him, so they always quarrelled. During those fights, the phrase "that woman" was constantly repeated. In time, Grace found out the truth.

At one of his earlier postings, Grace's father had a relationship with his secretary, a woman many years his junior and the single mother of two small children. As the relationship progressed, Grace's father began to take financial responsibility over his lover and her children, such as paying for her rent and her children's school fees. Even when he was transferred to another town, he continued his illicit affair and the monetary support that came with it. As the mistress's children grew older so did their taste for the good life. Their mother made sure they got it, bankrolled by her pliable man. The older child turned out to be the very same Nancy who tormented Grace in high school.

Years into what became a twelve-year relationship, Nancy's mother persuaded Grace's father to take a significantly large bank loan and build her a house on a plot he owned. With the debt taking most of his salary, he began to tinker with workplace funds to maintain his woman's unrelenting appetite for good things. In time, his actions caught up with him, leading to his sacking. Life went downhill from there. His lover wanted nothing to do with him then, and his wife and children could not hide their hostility towards him either.

All this came as a great shock to Grace. Again and again, her high school experiences played in her mind. She could not come to terms with the fact that Nancy's flaunted lifestyle was made possible by her own father's finances, even as she, her siblings, and their mother endured great hardships. Her younger brother had even dropped out midway through high school and wasted away in alcohol, trying to drown his frustrations. These would never have happened but for their father's infidelity.

Chapter Four

Grace has done well for herself now. She does everything to help her mother and siblings. However, one thing she finds extremely difficult to do is to trust men, especially concerning money. Her worst nightmare is to have somebody in her life who fails to provide financial support and channels her own hard-earned money into strangers' bank accounts.

All about Financial Infidelity

Your past affects your reaction to present situations. One area marked by your upbringing is your view of money. Because of your previous experiences, especially in childhood, you may not trust anyone else with it. Or you do as you please and so engage in binge shopping. Or you believe secrecy rules where money is concerned, so you do not tell anyone about your bank accounts and investments. Or you feel responsible for your extended family's school fees and are obliged to pay for them, too.

Often, two people get married, holding opposite expectations about finances. When they each insist on sticking to their respective positions, their relationship can slowly fall apart. Everyone knows sexual infidelity can destroy marriage, but financial infidelity can be just as destructive. Financial infidelity is the act of spending family money or committing to financial obligations without the knowledge of your partner. This includes opening bank accounts or borrowing money without your partner's knowledge. Financial infidelity also involves hiding personal assets from your spouse. Fights that ensue from such scenarios can be vicious and affect the intimacy you have with your partner at every level, which, in turn, can lead to anger and resentment.

Financial infidelity ranks as one of the major reasons for divorce. A recent survey shows its prevalence is even much higher than that of sexual infidelity. When you discover it, you experience a sense of betrayal and pain. However, as critical as the issue of finances is, most couples do not discuss it before they exchange vows. While some neglect to talk about money because they do not know better, a good number deliberately avoid the subject. Their excuse? "Money is a stressful subject. Every time we talk about it, it affects our romance, so we choose to avoid the topic." This is where many couples get it wrong. Money matters must be discussed and each issue arising ought to be addressed. Every couple heading for the altar should exhaustively deliberate over their financial positions and views. They have to reveal existing financial obligations, especially involving extended family. If you neglect to do this, the consequences can be devastating, as Mary and James found out.

Mary and James had been married for the last twelve years and they each managed a separate personal account. However, they did have a joint savings account for the children's education. Both deposited equal amounts of money in it every month. Everything was running well until Mary discovered something appalling by accident. James had defaulted on his commitment for six months and had somehow withdrawn and spent all their savings . . . and worse was to come. She also learned that their house mortgage was in arrears for thirteen months and had accrued penalties. There was a demand note giving fourteen-day notice to them to settle the debt or face foreclosure. I leave you to imagine where that left her marriage and what she felt towards her husband at that point.

Mary is not alone. Many others have found themselves in her situation, dealing with shocking revelations about their spouses. One case of financial infidelity is enough to ruin a relationship built over many years. The good news here is that you can know if your partner is involved in financial infidelity from telltale signs. The following are red flags to watch out for. Any one of them should raise your concern about your partner's financial faithfulness:

1. Unwillingness to discuss finances
2. Lies about income and expenditure
3. Dishonesty about purchases
4. Money withdrawal from joint accounts without any notification
5. Secrecy about bank accounts, investment group memberships, or credit cards
6. Need to control finances without any of or her own contribution
7. Overacting to every conversation on money

How to Handle Financial Infidelity

As with all marital issues, some financial matters need to be addressed before marriage; others, in the course of the union. One of the most important money conversations you need to have before marriage is how to pay for expenses and who is responsible for what bills. What about your personal money? These are all valid questions that you and your partner should answer together.

Who takes on the responsibility of paying bills and handling financial matters is a question of convenience and/or expertise. You may have more time and expertise to handle these aspects of the marriage or you could just be more responsible. Sharing control of your finances with another person means compromise and trust, which can be difficult even with someone you have known for a long time. One thing is sure: Men and women view money differently. Women see it as a means of security, while men view it as a source of power and status. Sadly, the latter sometimes choose to use such power to keep their partners down and needy.

The following are important ingredients of financial harmony in marriage:

1. **Discuss money at the onset of your relationship.** Different people have different views about money, so discuss such matters early on. It will help you understand your partner's spending habits, values, and attitudes. In turn, he will know the same about you, including your orientation about money growing up.

2. **Come clean on any liabilities.** It may not be unusual for you to have debts and other liabilities without disclosing the same to your spouse. You consider it your business and work towards handling it. It could be a car loan, a mortgage, an unpaid credit card, a student loan, or various other bills. When you get married, he may become directly responsible for your debts, so you have to tell him. Be candid in the discussion. There is nothing to be ashamed of. If you do not share it, it can come up when you least expect it and bite you. Yes, you may be uncomfortable about sharing your financial mistakes, but it is necessary if you want to establish a plan to take care of it.

3. **Have a joint financial plan.** A joint financial plan that includes a family budget and a monthly expense tracker puts you both on the same page. You each know what

your common financial goals and needs are, the general direction to achieve them, and the specific steps to take to succeed together. Make a list of your individual short and long-term goals. Have your partner do the same. Then come together and make a list of short and long-term goals together. Notice the similarities on your individual and combined lists and begin making financial preparations to accomplish those goals.

4. **Be open about your spending habits.** When you have any doubt about your partner's financial integrity, money-related disagreements can arise. You can develop trust by being open to each other about your respective spending habits and experiences with money. Do not assume that getting married means you have to merge all your finances. At the earliest convenience, ensure that there is clarity on these issues.

5. **Make financial decisions together.** Ensure that you and your spouse have equal knowledge and say in all decisions regarding family finances. All expenditure, savings, and investments should be arrived at by mutual agreement.

6. **Have quarterly structured financial meetings to evaluate and plan.** It is not enough to decide on your finances together. You must review your decisions regularly to assess your progress and to maintain accountability.

7. **Consider "his", "hers", and "ours" financial plans.** Create opportunities for separate financial plans alongside joint ones. You may each have a gift or passion for something that your partner is neither interested in nor excited about. Give each other leeway to pursue such pastimes because it contributes to your respective self-actualisation and, possibly, an increase in family finances.

Financial fidelity is crucial to any partnership, so secrets about money erode the trust that should bind it. How is your relationship with your partner as far as money matters go? Do you openly discuss them with one another or do you find it difficult to open up about your respective income and expenditure? Do you make financial decisions together about small and big investments? Your answers to these questions can help you evaluate your financial fidelity.

If money is not a topic you can talk about openly, then you may need to find a way to begin doing so. Open communication about financial commitments can help avert financial infidelity. It may not be uncommon today for you or your spouse to commit financially to certain things without the knowledge or consent of the other. You should stop that practice as it may lead to the breakup of your marriage. Talk about money and do not be a statistic.

Reflection

For every animal in the forest is Mine and the cattle on a thousand hills. (Psalm 50:10)

"Suppose one of you wants to build a tower. Won't you first sit down and estimate the cost to see if you have enough money to complete it?" (Luke 14:28)

If any of you lacks wisdom, he should ask God, who gives generously to all without finding fault, and it will be given to him. (James 1:5)

Chapter Five

No Dirty Laundry in Public

Bilhah and her husband Julius had not spoken much to each other in three weeks and the stalemate shows no signs of thawing. It all started when she felt a tiny lump in her left breast while showering, which immediately alarmed her. She called Julius at his work and informed him of her discovery. They agreed to meet in town and to see a doctor together.

The doctor examined the lump but could not give them a definite diagnosis without exhaustive tests, so he sent them to the lab for a biopsy. With the sample on its way for testing, the couple took the rest of the day off and went home to take it all in. Neither said much to the other.

In the days that followed, Bilhah became irritable and withdrawn. Even in the best of days, to begin with, she was never keen to share with anyone what went on in her mind and heart. She refused to talk about the situation hanging over their heads. Whenever Julius tried to say something encouraging, she remained unresponsive. When he persisted, she lashed out. After a while, he let her be.

Unable to talk to his wife about her condition, he reached out to friends close to Bilhah and himself to let them know their situation. They became his solace. Whenever the burden

Chapter Five

became too heavy, he shared about it to them and they provided hope and comfort. One evening, they turned up unannounced at the couple's house. They all had tea and small talk together for an hour or so. When they were about to leave, they offered to pray for Julius and Bilhah, especially for her biopsy results to come back negative.

As soon as they said amen, Bilhah bolted out of the sitting room and went to the bedroom, in tears. Neither Julius nor the visitors read anything strange in her behaviour, so they carried on. Julius walked the friends to their own car. Upon returning to the house, he switched on the TV to watch the news. His experience had taught him to leave Bilhah alone when she was upset and to wait until she was ready to talk. When he finally entered their bedroom, Bilhah's first words were, "How could you?"

"How could I what?" asked a confused Julius.

"How could you tell everyone about my condition? You have no right to discuss about me with our friends. What do you know about the possibility of cancer? For you, it's just another story to share with everyone."

This was not the first time Julius and Bilhah had argued about his "betrayal" of her confidence by sharing domestic issues outside the walls of their home. In their last big fight, Bilhah had lost her job and, in an attempt to help her, Julius had asked his friends to let him know about any employment opportunities for her. When she found out about his SOS on her behalf, she hit the roof. "I can find a job for myself. Don't go around looking for a godfather to help me out. Next time, don't try to assist me when I don't ask for it."

The experience left Julius confused and angry. No matter how hard he tried, he could not see where he had gone wrong. He could not understand how telling their close friends constituted a breach of confidence. He had grown up knowing that a problem shared was a problem half-solved. He had been brought up to holler for aid when the burden became too heavy. On the other hand, his wife was from the opposite side of town. She had been spanked and severely reprimanded for telling a playmate that her big brother had been expelled from school for leading a riot. She learned painfully that her family did not let outsiders in on their domestic issues. Those matters remained within the walls of their home and there were no exceptions.

When the biopsy results came back, the growth was declared benign, but it still needed to be removed. Surgery was scheduled almost immediately. Although friends called constantly for updates, Julius did not tell them anything for fear of stirring up another round of anger and accusations, if one of them slipped up and called her. However, in spite of his precautions, Julius still ended up in another incident with Bilhah.

During a follow-up meeting with the doctor, the physician asked Bilhah about her family's medical history, especially concerning cancer. She told him they had none, but Julius reminded her about her mother's sister. Her aunt had been diagnosed with the disease but had beaten it. Bilhah became visibly upset at her husband. As soon as they left the clinic, she ranted at Julius for telling the specialist. "How many times do we have to go through this? I don't talk about your family, so don't talk about mine to others."

Chapter Five

Julius was stunned. He could not believe that Bilhah had withheld vital information for any reason other than forgetfulness. How could that fact shared with the doctor be an intrusion of her privacy? He threw up his arms in despair.

Why Confidentiality Is Important in Marriage

Confidentiality is the right of an individual to have personal, identifiable information kept private. It is an essential part of any healthy relationship. Consistent communication can occur only when both parties feel comfortable and safe enough to share their innermost selves with each other without fear of trust being broken. Any confidential info shared between spouses must be guarded. Sharing it with a third party is not only dishonourable but also destructive to the marriage. If you must confide in someone, do so to a neutral third party such as a marriage counsellor or a church minister.

There are two ways in which sharing confidential information from your marriage can go terribly wrong. One, you lose control of the information. Two, you drop your objectivity.

You lose control of the information once you break confidentiality. When you relay private info to a third party, that third party can choose to share it with other people without your knowledge. You run the risk of becoming a topic of conversation among your friends and family. It can be embarrassing and can worsen your marital issues or create new ones where none existed.

You drop your objectivity when you share confidential information. Your well-being is your friends' and family's primary concern. Sharing about ill health or other bad news may create panic among them and not solve problems. You and your spouse may already be struggling to cope with your own emotions about the matter on hand. Adding those of others into the mix, sympathetic as they may be, may simply weigh you down. Trying to anticipate their reactions can lead to your increased stress, anxiety, and fear.

Bilhah had not yet come to terms with the possibility of breast cancer, yet Julius had already roped in his friends to pray for her. His was a very noble motive, but it represented a challenge to Bilhah and their relationship in general. She was still trying to deal with shock, denial, and anger; she did not need to be the focus of other people's attention in coping with all that.

How to Tell Others about Your Situation

Difficult as it may be, you must discuss this matter with your spouse. Be sensitive and rational. As a couple, it is important to agree on who should be involved, especially among your family and friends. Consider the manner of sharing your information. If you allow others to share your news, they might be able to alleviate your awkwardness in telling it yourself.

Though you may want to announce to everyone you know, it may be best to tell only those who are a positive source of strength and support in your life, e.g., a close friend or two and, of course, immediate family members. The extended family and distant others can be informed later, once you and your spouse are strong enough to handle them and only if you both agree to do so. Everyone processes challenges in their own peculiar way, so respect the timing of your partner. Bilhah felt disrespected and greatly injured because Julius violated her privacy—and more than once!

As you plan to share confidential information to others, also consider how much of it you wish to share. For example, it may be helpful to begin with a simple prayer request for your spouse's condition. Get down to the nitty-gritty when the time is right and everyone is ready for it. If you do not have all the information yet, then hold off from sharing until you do. Unless you have all the facts straightened out, wait before you share. If you have an opinion different from that of your spouse's, use negotiation skills to agree.

Do not concern yourself with what others think of you and your decisions. Well-meaning friends can offer advice and anecdotes, but it is still your spouse's and your joint choice that matters. You can also let your support group know what you need from them to avoid being smothered by their opinions and attention. Keep them posted as everything becomes clearer.

Honesty Is Still the Best

If you are dealing with a dire predicament, how do you break the news to your children, family, and friends? You may be apprehensive about their reaction, so your natural response may be to protect them from the pain or shock.

When talking with your children, honesty is still best. You need to consider their ages and apply wisdom, depending on their respective level of understanding. You may want to consult with a child psychologist or a similar professional before disclosing the news to them because your children need support. They also need to be honest with their own feelings without fear of hurting you. You may need some coaching to be effective in communicating the realities of the situation to them.

You can try to hide the truth from your kids, but when they start seeing its effects, they can end up confused. Most children are not yet able to put pieces together, so let them see the big picture. They may pick things up from the media or other people, so be careful about discussing the situation in a way they can understand. You can choose exactly how little or much you want to share with them. Be optimistic. Also be there for them, when they want to talk. Reassure the kids of your love for them. However, in the initial stages, you may choose not to involve them, if they are too young to come to terms with the intensity of the matter and its possible outcomes. Apply discernment and wisdom.

If you are the afflicted partner, your spouse would also have his own struggles. He might go through a sense of possible loss and grief, which should not be ignored. You should support one another as a couple and agree on your immediate support system. No disclosure should happen without mutual agreement and readiness to handle the same.

If the confidential information you intend to share with others is as grave as, say, a diagnosis of cancer, know that it will be life-altering for everyone: family, friends, and even colleagues. It should be handled with the care and sensitivity it requires. Expect a flood of emotions. You may not feel prepared for this journey, but you have to take it. The key here is honest communication. Find avenues that will allow your family members to express themselves. Hold meetings with them. Share your fears with a close friend.

Before you decide to tell people your confidential information, do consider the following:

1. What kind of relationship do you have with these people? What are the pros and cons of sharing your news with them?
2. Do they have particular issues that can affect their ability to support you?
3. What are their attitudes and knowledge about your situation?
4. Why do you want to disclose to them in particular? What kind of support can they provide?
5. For each person you want to tell, ask yourself if the person needs to know now.

You may wonder just how much you should disclose to your partner or significant others and the appropriate time to do so. Be sensitive and comfortable about your level of disclosure.

Self-Disclosure

Self-disclosure reveals information about a person that is unknown to others. Sometimes, individuals have legitimate reasons for managing privacy instead of disclosing information. Self-disclosure is a risky but necessary part of building and maintaining healthy relationships.

You may have a strong level of self-disclosure, but the communication process is thwarted if your spouse chooses not to listen or to engage with you at any level. It is unfortunate when you discover something about him through a third party. It would be best to put your fears behind you and talk freely. Lack of self-disclosure has consequences and results in lost trust, the main ingredient for holding relationships together.

Good, open communication is the top need in marriage. Nothing is as easy as talking; nothing is as difficult as communicating. Using words correctly and skilfully is an important part of communication, but it is even more important that you and your husband are willing to communicate in ways that result in deeper honesty and openness.

Effective communication begins with transparency. Transparency in marriage is illustrated in Genesis 2:25 as follows: "Adam and his wife were both naked, and they felt no shame." However, after their fall from grace, "Then the eyes of both of them were opened, and they realised they were naked, so they sewed fig leaves together and made coverings for themselves" (Genesis 3:7).

You might be one of those people who spend tremendous time and energy building façades to hide your insecurities. You are afraid that, if someone finds out who you really are, you will be rejected. Men in particular are threatened by deep and honest communication. So the scenario is that many wives and many husbands are afraid to be honest with each other.

At the same time, Scripture warns about being too open and honest. Proverbs 10:19 says, "Sin is not ended by multiplying words, but the prudent hold their tongues." The saying "sticks and stones may break my bones, but words can never hurt me" is not true. Words *can* hurt. They cut, rip, and wound. "Rash language cuts and maims, but there is healing in the words of the wise" (Proverbs 12:18). If you use words rashly, then you would do well to "hold your tongue".

Deep communication takes a long time to achieve. You and your spouse need to be headed in that direction. In the same way you learn and sharpen most skills, start at an easy level and work your way toward proficiency in communication. When you and your spouse reach the transparency level, you can operate as one. Reaching that level is not easy, but the rewards far outweigh the cost because we all long deeply to be heard and understood. The most natural place for this to occur is within the safe harbour of a healthy marriage. That safe harbour can be created and maintained only by a couple committed to each other in love. It is a covenant. First John 4:18 describes the commitment that brings freedom: "Perfect love drives out fear."

Whatever you do, do not wash your dirty linen in public. Simply remember not to discuss intimate family matters "out there", especially if they are personal and without the consent of your partner.

Reflection

Come to me, all you who are weary and burdened, and I will give you rest. Take my yoke upon you and learn from me, for I am gentle and humble in heart, and you will find rest for your souls. For my yoke is easy and my burden is light. (Matthew 11:28-30)

Chapter Six

Someone Else Has My Back

"All I did was to help my husband become the great man he once was," Liz explained. "Now I don't know whether I have a marriage or not."

For the first four years of their marriage, Tim was everything she desired in a mate. He was simple and down to earth. If he was not at work, he was home or at their church. He was very close to his extended family. Liz's own family loved him a lot and he got along very well with each of them. He was very pleasant to have around. He had a way of making Liz laugh. But then he lost his job.

Tim believed in doing the right thing. He refused to be part of anything that was not above board, so when he unearthed shady practices at work that cost his company millions of Kenyan shillings, he pursued the matter with zeal. Instead of being rewarded, he was hounded out of the company after more than ten years of faithful service. It took him a while to accept all that, but when it finally did sink in, he became a constantly angry man. He stayed at home all day, seething. Liz learned when to say something to him and when to stay out of his way. If she got her timings wrong, he exploded. When he was not angry, he would fall into depression and stay in bed for days.

Chapter Six

Liz deeply missed the lively husband she knew him to be. Tim had just recently talked excitedly about their next few years together. Now, he believed life was unfair and all good people lost in the end. With his ability and experience, he could have easily found another job, but he was not ready to start from the bottom and possibly lose everything along the way. Concerned for Tim, Liz called together his mother and his siblings, so they could do an intervention for him.

After lengthy discussions, they all agreed to raise a substantial amount of money to fund a business that Tim could start himself. He would be his own boss and control his own destiny. As they talked, Bea's name came up. She was a friend of Tim's sister and was a successful entrepreneur. Like Tim, she had a fruitful career cut short unjustly. She had gone through the same depression and anger as Tim had, but she learned to direct her frustration towards a business start-up. She had since distinguished herself as a businesswoman. Everyone agreed she would be a good person to help Tim see his situation differently and discover new opportunities for himself.

Initially, Tim was not enthusiastic about the arrangement. He resented the fact that the family had stepped in to intervene. However, after much persuasion, he half-heartedly agreed to give it a try. Liz was present at his first meeting with Bea. She was excited that her husband and Bea had connected. He had actually laughed for the first time in weeks. He wanted to hear more from Bea.

That night, Tim talked to his wife at length—something which had not happened since his sacking. He went over the things he had discussed with Bea and expressed optimism that he could rise up again and put his life back on track. He saw nothing but an opportunity to prove he could be something in spite of his bad experience.

Over the next few weeks, Tim and Bea met often to put together his action plan. They also talked on the phone constantly. He updated Liz about their discussions. At first, she shared in her husband's enthusiasm, but then she began to notice something that made her uncomfortable. In the beginning, Tim talked a lot about the business opportunity while giving Bea credit for opening his eyes. Then he began to focus less on the professional and more on the personal as he discussed Bea. He thought her a great person.

Liz did not give it too much thought, especially when her husband's business took off. All she cared about was the return of Tim and their old life. But that never happened. A year down the line, he had clearly done very well for himself. He more than got back on his feet financially. His confidence also returned but appeared to border on cockiness. And all he talked about was Bea and his business.

Liz had no reason to believe anything untoward happening between Tim and Bea, but he acted as though he owed everything to her. If he needed to discuss anything, he called Bea. Sometimes, when he looked troubled and Liz asked how he was, he would say, "It's okay. I'll talk to Bea. She will sort me out." When she tried to bring up her frustration over his closeness with the businesswoman, Tim accused her of unfounded jealousy and insecurity.

Chapter Six

Emotional Intimacy

Emotional intimacy is the closeness created through shared feelings. Emotional intimacy can be expressed in verbal and nonverbal communication. Emotional intimacy can be shared, not just with your partner in life, but with friends, family, and colleagues. It might involve the disclosure of feelings and emotions in order to reach an understanding, and offer mutual support to one another. The first step towards emotional awareness and expression is to assess your feelings, identify them, and recognise the possible reasons for them. Notice the differences between strong emotions, e.g., terror and fury, and subtle ones, e.g., anxiety, insecurity, and irritation. Emotional intimacy can occur when you and another person know your feelings and the means to convey them to each other. You both also know how best to express mutual concern and understanding.

On the other hand, emotional infidelity is your spouse's or your behaviour when either of you engage in emotional intimacy with someone other than each other. Secrecy is usually maintained when there is a clear shared attraction. Any situation that causes some degree of emotional unavailability on your spouse's or your part and interferes with the quality of your relationship is also considered emotional infidelity. You might justify it by saying that it is neither sexual nor physical. While it may be characterised by perfectly harmless business lunches and "innocently flirtatious" communication, the fact remains: it creates emotional distance in the marriage.

Emotional connections can happen in person or a distant relationship via the phone or on Internet. Tim and Bea obviously got into an emotional relationship by spending time together, which threatened Tim's own intimacy with Liz. But how dangerous is emotional infidelity to a marriage? Very dangerous because it takes away time and energy from the marriage and can lead to sexual infidelity. In turn, the latter may result in the end of a union.

Emotional infidelity is a symptom of problems already existing in a marriage. When the primary relationship is not emotionally and physically intimate, you make yourself vulnerable to infidelity: emotional, physical, or both. It is therefore prudent to deal with the underlying problems.

It is easy to fall into emotional infidelity because you do it with someone with whom you have no shared responsibility, such as money, children, or household chores. You can reveal your deepest feelings with that person and there will be no opportunity for conflict. You can feel good with him because you do not live together; you do not know each other's negatives. You think he is wonderful. But all that is an easy way out of dealing with the real issues.

The primary problem that leads to emotional infidelity is emotional distance between spouses. While emotional infidelity is a symptom of emotional distance within the primary relationship, the emotional distance itself is a symptom of deeper issues within the marriage. When one partner becomes emotionally attached to someone else the relationship suffers lack of intimacy, trust, and oneness. It simply means that the relationship is suffering from a vacuum of emptiness, poor communication and lack of intimacy. The negativity and attitude that one adopts finds it easier to invest emotionally elsewhere as opposed to working on a relationship that they may consider a waste of time.

Chapter Six

It is helpful to acknowledge some signs that serve as warning of an emotional relationship:

"We are just friends" is always your excuse. This rationale allows you to make excuses about something you know is no longer legitimate or honest. You keep it a secret, which is itself a warning sign. Secrets create an unhealthy bond and, subsequently, a false sense of emotional safety and trust with the person. It rips away your trust and suspicion creeps in. You lose out on intimacy with your spouse this way.

You regard your "friend" as a confidant. When you share confidential matters, your hopes and aspirations, fears and passions, and problems with each other, you deepen your intimacy. This leads to the creation of an emotional bond between the two of you. It is time taken away from your marriage.

You discuss your spouse with your "friend". Talking about your spouse and details of your marriage, e.g., what your partner lacks or what you are not getting, sends the wrong signal. It shows that you are lonely, needy, and ready for a love relationship with the other person, who seems to understand you better.

You cannot get the "friend" out of your mind. Every time you think about the person, you want to make an impression in word and deed. You become very particular about how you dress up, what you do, and how you do it in front of her. You cannot wait to connect with her, without sharing the details with your spouse. You are caught in the web! You begin to fantasise about a love or sexual relationship with the other person. Wet dreams become frequent.

You justify your "friendship" because, after all, you do not have sex with each other. It always appears innocent; however, as the bond grows, it takes a simple touch for the spark to ignite. Before you know it, both of you are deep in a sexual relationship.

You send gifts to each other unnecessarily. Gifts are a powerful language of love and the choices of gifts speak volumes. And you do not tell your spouse about them at all. Gifts send clear messages that you are intimate and are a "we" and have an "ours". Beyond gifts, you spend quality time with each other, exchange words of affirmation, and do acts of service for one another.

Where You Stand: A Self-Assessment

Why waste a wonderful relationship by not dealing with your fears, controlling patterns, and self-abandonment now, in your marriage? Instead of looking for someone else to fill your emptiness and to take away your loneliness, why not learn to do them for yourself so you can break your dysfunction and become the loving human being you are? Imagine the wonderful marriage you both can have, if you both learned to be responsible for your own feelings and ability to love.

Like most of us, you have friends of the opposite sex. They may be colleagues, casual acquaintances, or close confidants. But here is the question: how close can you get without falling over the precipice? Here are some signs to watch out for:

Are you spending too much time with someone other than your spouse? You may be spending inappropriate or excessive time with someone else, time that should rightfully be spent with family. You may become too comfortable and begin to share intimate feelings with the other person rather than with your spouse. You might confide more in your "friend", leaving no room for your spouse. Any time you invest more emotions and time into a relationship other than your marriage, you threaten the latter.

Are you keeping your spouse in the dark about a "friendship"? You are not open to your spouse about the amount of time you spend with the "friend". You might tell him that you are busy at work while actually meeting the "friend". Or you might be avoiding any mention of your "friend" while discussing the day's activities. You fail to mention a coffee date. So why are you hiding such details from your spouse? Even if no physical intimacy occurs, your deception shows something is wrong, which can undermine your marriage.

Is your partner overly critical of you? When you become emotionally involved with a third party, more often than not, you start finding fault with your spouse and disrespecting him. You then cause a strain in your marriage.

What is your motive? When you dress up for the day with a particular person in mind other than your spouse, it is a clear sign you are developing an emotional intimacy with someone else. Your communications are increasingly devoted to that person and you cannot wait to check your phone to see the latest text from your "friend". You are up in the middle of the night to respond to any messages. When the balance of contact tips away from your spouse, it is a sure sign of trouble.

Although your "friendship" begins on a purely platonic level, sexual and emotional chemistries can present themselves. They could lead to physical intimacy, if nurtured. Be true to yourself and faithful to your spouse.

You cannot talk about emotional intimacy without the issue of infidelity coming up. Infidelity is not always sexual; many times, it is emotional infidelity. Much energy, time, and money can be spent with someone else whom you see more often than you should. Such relationships are often justified by the fact that a sexual relationship does not exist. Infidelity can also take place when you handle finances without any accountability and in a manner that puts your family at risk.

Marriage has its challenges, but few compare to the monumental task of healing from infidelity. As a marriage counsellor, I have heard clients confess that the discovery of an infidelity was the lowest, darkest moment of their entire lives. Because illicit affairs shatter trust, many seriously contemplate an end to their marriages. However, it is important to know that, no matter how bleak things seem, it is possible to revitalise a marriage wounded by unfaithfulness. Years of interactions with clients in committed, loving unions have taught me definite patterns to follow to bring marriages back from the brink of disaster.

If unhappiness with your spouse contributed to your decision to have an affair, you need to address your feelings honestly, so you both can make changes. If open communication is a problem, consider seeking help from a qualified marriage therapist or taking a communication skills class.

As important as it is to discuss what happened, talking about the infidelity should not be the only thing you do. Couples who successfully rebuild their marriages recognise the importance of spending time together, talking about their difficulties without dwelling on painful topics. They intentionally create opportunities to reconnect and nurture their relationship.

Chapter Six

Ultimately, the key to healing from infidelity is forgiveness. This is often the last step in the healing process. Say, your spouse was unfaithful to you and is now doing his best to do everything right: confess, repent, listen, and earn trust again, but your marriage still will not mend unless you, the betrayed, forgive him. In turn, he must also forgive himself. Forgiveness reopens the door to true intimacy and connection.

Forgiveness does not happen out of thin air. It can result only from a conscious decision to stop the blame game, make peace, and start afresh with a clean slate. If the past has had you in its clutches, take the next step to have more love in your life: decide to forgive today.

Reflection

Create in me a pure heart, O God, and renew a steadfast spirit within me. Do not cast me from your presence or take your Holy Spirit from me. Restore to me the joy of your salvation and grant me a willing spirit, to sustain me. Then I will teach transgressors your ways, so that sinners will turn back to you. (Psalm 51:10-13)

No temptation has overtaken you except what is common to mankind. And God is faithful; He will not let you be tempted beyond what you can bear. But when you are tempted, He will also provide a way out so that you can endure it. (1 Corinthians 10:13)

Chapter Seven

Kids Causing Troubled Waters

Lena and Jack had been married for six years. They had two sons born just over a year apart. Their marriage was generally peaceful except for one area in which they could not seem to agree: child discipline. They each were brought up in families that approached the matter in divergent ways.

In Lena's home, the father was the undisputed head of the household. He handled all matters and provided clear directions on how things were to be done. What could or could not be watched on TV was not only clearly set out but religiously enforced. Curfews were in place and study times were well established. Everyone knew what times to go to bed and to wake up.

Jack's family was the polar opposite to Lena's. His father was hardly at home. When he was around the house, he switched on the TV, stretched himself out on the sofa, and ordered everybody not to disturb him. He left the kids' discipline to his wife. Their house did not run by any set rules. Members came and went as they wished.

Lena got married to Jack with the knowledge that homes were run by defined rules placed and applied largely by the father. Jack, on the other hand, had a free-range mentality. If the kids wanted to watch cartoons all day long, he did not see any problem with that. If they wanted to stay up until midnight, he allowed them to do so, as long as they were quiet.

Lena did everything to get her husband to create order and purpose to the home but failed. Jack simply did not think rules were necessary, which exasperated his wife further. Meanwhile, their children's lack of discipline showed even in school. Every so often, the teacher wrote in their diaries that homework was either incomplete or sloppy. Once or twice, Lena and Jack were summoned to school to discuss various issues regarding the boys. Jack never took any of it seriously. He acted as though everyone was making a fuss over nothing. Clearly, there was no amicable solution in sight as Lena and Jack's arguments escalated.

Understanding Conflict in Marriage

Have you ever had a disagreement or misunderstanding with your spouse over simple matters, particularly over children and their discipline? Have you ever argued on what should or should not be done with them? If your answer is yes to either or both questions, then welcome to the real world! Unfortunately for you, there is no university on Earth that offers a degree in child rearing. You must use your own upbringing as a reference point, exercising discretion in what to apply to your own children. Use Scripture as a foundational basis. "Start children off on the way they should go and, even when they are old, they will not turn from it" (Proverbs 22:6).

While children are a joy, they do create conflict in marriages, which can drain and devastate an entire family if constant and mishandled. However, since conflict is inevitable and normal in all healthy relationships, it is essential not to avoid it but to address it. After all, two people cannot always agree on everything. Rather than side-step conflict altogether, especially that concerning kids, you must first understand what it is really all about.

Conflict arises from differences or disagreements over preferences, values, or beliefs. To you, these differences may seem trivial, but your spouse may not share the same sentiment. When a conflict triggers strong emotions on his part, an unmet personal need may be likely at the core of the problem. The need may be for safety and security, respect and appreciation, or closeness and intimacy. In many instances, the conflict may simply be because of a communication breakdown, unrealistic expectations, or a power struggle. Your orientation, attitudes, experiences, personality, or worldview can also be sources of it.

In spite of the challenges it poses, conflict can provide an opportunity for personal growth when handled well. After all, everyone seeks love, understanding, respect, and support even in the midst of a marital fight. What is important is that you and your spouse should be willing to compromise even when you each feel injured. Lack of sensitivity may result in irreconcilable differences that can lead to separation. The following are more facts to know about conflict:

Your perception of the conflict is always subjective, not objective. Your perceptions are influenced by your entire life experience, which your partner may not necessarily share. Be patient and understanding, and find the common ground that you both can work with.

Conflict festers when ignored. Deal with issues promptly because delays bring about resentment, distance, and a vacuum in the relationship. When these scenarios continue for a long time, they can result in a lack of intimacy.

Chapter Seven

Conflict can be minimised or avoided altogether, if you voice your expectations. In relationships, agreements are often implied rather than clearly stipulated. You may assume your husband knows what you want, so you expect certain responses that may not, in fact, be forthcoming. Be sure to speak out not only to your spouse but to your entire household. Everybody needs to know what you expect of them. It is the only way they can tell whether or not they are living up to your expectations.

Conflict is best ended by letting go of offences and moving on. Do not dwell on the offence. Keeping a record of wrongs is not an option. Learn to forgive and let go. It is the only way you can enjoy peace and contentment.

Correct Ways to Respond to Conflict

In time, the initial excitement of marriage gives way to responsibilities. With children to raise, bills to pay, and work to accomplish, your stress is bound to build up because they all tap into the energy you once set aside to sustain romance in the marriage. All that tension can contribute to conflicts. Since they are unavoidable, here are ways for you to follow in order to address them and achieve the best outcome:

1. Always try to stay calm, regardless of the conflict. It is not easy to deal with the challenge, when you are angry or in some other state of heightened emotion. Reduce the intensity of your reactions and formulate your thoughts and feelings into clear, nonthreatening "I" statements, e.g., "I feel that you're not listening to me, when I'm talking about the children's welfare with you."

2. Pick your battles wisely. Not every battle is worth fighting. There are conflicts you can avoid. Deal with the issues at hand and avoid bringing up the past. It is never a fair fight when you dredge up history and confront your spouse with it.
3. Acknowledge your selfish desires and set them aside. Instead, have your spouse's interest at heart.
4. Communicate clearly and specifically about your needs and desires all the time.
5. Remember that you are fighting a friend, not an enemy. Apply some compassion and tenderness even in the midst of the conflict.

Finding Common Ground in Parenting

With that groundwork about conflict in general, you can now focus specifically on parenting, a common trigger of marital fights. When parenting, you and your spouse must know the difference between having dissimilar beliefs and communication styles, and being unable to agree on *decisions* regarding your children.

Since you and your husband are not the same people, you each have your own style of relating to your kids. While you might be very chatty with them, your spouse might be more reserved. Both styles are okay; it is the differences around parental *decisions concerning children, which* can cause problems.

For example, you believe your children should be punished harshly for lying. On the other hand, your spouse thinks it is not a big deal. As a result, you both are not on the same page when it comes to the consequences of their actions. Here is the truth: kids can infer when their parents are not in sync over certain matters. When they feel your lack of unity, they can develop a sense of instability. Sometimes, they can also use it to provoke a fight between you and your spouse.

Disagreements between parents can cause minor flare-ups or an all-out war in your household. The following guidelines offered by experts can help you avoid conflict when it comes to raising your children:

1. **Provide back-up.** Make it a rule that if one parent disciplines the kids, the other parent must back them up, even if they do not agree. If you do not do this, your children will think you are not a unified team, which undermines your authority. Your children will see that they can get around any parenting decision you make. However, this does not apply if either of you are involved in the neglect or abuse of your children. If you feel that your spouse's actions towards your children is detrimental to them in a physical or emotional way, then you need to put your foot down and disagree. Take the necessary steps to ensure your kids are safe.

2. **Be on the same page.** Find a way to arrive in the same place regarding your children. Be aware that your fights over their discipline disturb them. They do not like to see their parents disagreeing with each other. And understand that every time you argue over parenting, the focus shifts away from your children. When things are calm again and you are out of your children's earshot, discuss better ways of handling the situation with your spouse and then present a unified front.

3. **The more passionate parent makes the call over an issue.** If you and your spouse are on different pages and neither of you can cross over to the other side, then the parent who feels more passionately about the issue makes the judgement call. For example, your twelve-year-old wants to attend a sleepover at a good friend's house, but your spouse is fearful of giving your child that kind of independence at such an early age. You can say, "I feel strongly about this and I'd really like you to support me, even if you don't see it the same way."

4. **Discuss parenting decisions when you are calm.** You have a better shot at influencing your spouse's decision by calmly listening without being critical. There is no such thing as "one truth". There are many ways to think about things, not just your way. When you can be respectful of that and make room for your spouse's thoughts, different as they may be from your own, you have a chance of keeping him open to your way of thinking, too. Otherwise, your closed attitude can put him always on the defensive, which diverts you both from the real issue.

5. **Empathise with your child, but do not throw your spouse under the bus.** If your spouse feels more strongly about something and you have to go along with that decision, you can say to your child, "I know it's hard for you when I won't let you go on a sleepover. It bothers you because you feel you're already ready for this independence." You empathise with your child's feelings but do not break the unified stance. When you show empathy, your kid feels understood and not alone. Later, you can discuss your differing views with your spouse and perhaps come up with a better decision in the future.

6. **Know your spouse's family history.** It may be difficult for you to understand your spouse's perspective on child rearing because it is so different from your own. I recommend you knowing his family history and determining how deeply his beliefs are rooted. It may help you to see things more objectively and less personally, so you can respond with less prejudice. Help each other see that safety issues, environmental concerns, and cultural norms change over time. What might have worked back in both your childhoods might not make sense now. Anxiety about changes and differences can often cause parents with the best of intentions to stick to the familiar and comfortable, rather than to the best for the present situation.

7. **Do not let your children play you both against each other.** Sometimes, kids use your and your husband's different parenting styles to manipulate and set you against each other, so they can get off the hook. Do not let them. When kids provoke you to argue with your spouse, they do not get the discipline they need. They are not being held accountable. The tension between you and your spouse can spill over to the entire house, which can cause your child to act out.

8. **Take a timeout.** Rather than getting into a battle of who is right and who is wrong, focus on working on a plan together with your spouse. Take a timeout if you need one. Take a walk. Drive around a bit. Do something else. When you come back, set up a time to talk. You can say, "Let's each spend a few minutes talking about the issue. I'm just going to listen and not speak a word. I'm not going to interrupt you. Just let me hear why this is so important to you because you're not usually this passionate about things."

9. **Listen.** You should give each other a few minutes to talk about the issue under contention. Everyone has their own wishes, yearnings, traditions, and visions. If you can spend a few minutes just hearing each other out without stirring up aggression, defensiveness, or the blame game, you can find common ground from which to work together. What can you each do to negotiate on the matter?

10. **Seek professional help, when necessary, to mediate between you and your spouse.** Is it time for a counsellor to step in and work things out between the both of you? If you feel like you have tried everything and still cannot get on the same page with your partner, you may need some personal help. A good therapist will help you find ways to talk to each other without fighting over every parenting issue that comes up. There is no shame in this.

Believe it or not, natural differences between spouses can be treated as strengths, not causes of arguments. Differences can help you expand your own perspective to understand each other better. The bottom line: it is fine to have different communication styles and belief systems. No two people come together with the exact same opinions and values every single time. The important thing is to find a way to unite, so your kids are not torn up by your conflicts.

Reflection

Apply your heart to instruction and your ears to words of knowledge. Do not withhold discipline from a child; if you punish them with the rod, they will not die. Punish them with the rod and save them from death. (Proverbs 23:12-14)

Fathers, do not embitter your children or they will become discouraged. (Colossians 3:21)

Chapter Eight

No Longer the Man He Was

Joy noticed something was amiss with Joe as he began to withdraw and even get irritated when touched in a suggestive way. This was unusual behaviour for a man once sexually indefatigable. At first, she accepted his explanations: He was tired. He was stressed. He needed time to himself. She gave him the space he requested, but it did nothing to make their situation better.

The few occasions Joy managed to get Joe to make love to her, everything happened quickly and impersonally. Naturally, she began to worry and that worry turned into fear. Was he seeing someone else? Did he no longer find her attractive? Unable to live with her fears and afraid to ask him directly, she wrote him a note, expressing her feelings and wondering if she was doing anything wrong.

When Joe came home that evening and read her message, he was livid. He accused her of obsessing about sex and adding to his problems instead of helping him through it. She had cooked his favourite dinner, but he refused to eat that night and went to bed early. Joe's angry outburst was unlike him, so Joy was now certain something was indeed wrong. Unsure about what to do next, she did what her husband did; she withdrew into her own world and worked herself to the bone. When it all became too heavy to bear, she just sat on her bed and cried.

Chapter Eight

One day, the whole thing became clear to Joy when she met her best friend Jeanette over coffee. In the course of their conversation, the latter divulged a private discussion between Joe and her husband. "I'm not supposed to tell you this, but I see that you've not been yourself lately. I think I know why." Joe had confided to Dan about his problem with erectile dysfunction and his refusal to see a doctor about his condition. He had also expressed fear that their marriage was heading for the rocks, but he did not know what to do. Instead, Joe found himself getting angrier every day with life and with everybody.

While Joy was relieved to know the truth, she had no idea what to do about it. Bringing it up with Joe might make him angry again. She was also concerned that she may have caused his condition.

The Place of Sexual Fulfilment in Marriage

Many researchers conclude that the number one expectation of men in a marriage is sexual fulfilment. It is assumed that they are always primed for sex. Sadly, this is nothing but a myth. In popular and scientific dialogues, little is ever mentioned about male sexual difficulties and the negative effects they have on marital relationships, but Joy is not alone in her experience. Many other women suffer in silence with husbands who show little or no interest in sex.

Generally, men do not discuss this topic to protect their egos. They prefer either to fight or to flee, living in denial rather than dealing with the situation. For survival, many blame it on their wives, using the avoidance-and-blame game. This can cause a lot of pain and frustration to you, if such is the scenario in your bedroom. If not addressed, it can even destroy your marriage. Whatever the case may be, this state of affairs must not go on indefinitely without resolution because it has the potential to destroy you both and your relationship.

Sex is an integral part of a healthy marriage. In many cases, it is the glue that binds you and your spouse together in the initial stages of your relationship. However, sex can also be the reason for conflicts. When couples fight and do not agree on anything, check their sex life. It has a way of breeding resentment, rejection, and rebellion, which often opens the door to infidelity.

Confronting Erectile Dysfunction

There are many things to discuss about sex and sexual fulfilment in marriage. Various books are available in the market doing just that. In this book, however, I focus primarily on the issue of erectile dysfunction. Erectile dysfunction is defined as the failure to have or to maintain an erection sufficient for satisfying sex. Although many do not admit it, it affects a good proportion of the male population. Many men, young and old alike, suffer from this condition, but less than ten percent of those affected seek medical attention. The rest continue to live in silence or denial, preventing them and their partners from having any sexual fulfilment.

Most men make enough testosterone to maintain libido throughout their lives. However, a study indicated that, on average, testosterone levels fall by about one percent every year after age forty-five. Generally, therefore, erectile dysfunction increases as men grow old, with fifty-two percent of them, from ages forty-five to seventy, having some degree of sexual dysfunction.

Chapter Eight

Studies indicate that erectile dysfunction, as with most sexual problems, is seventy percent a physical issue and thirty percent, psychological. The physical aspect may be caused by an accident, hormones, another medical condition (e.g., diabetes, kidney disease, or hardened arteries), or lifestyle choices (e.g., drug abuse, alcoholism, obesity). The debilitation results in your husband having to deal with fear, shame, guilt, and frustration because it affects his ego. It is not unusual for someone in his position to become angry and resentful, blaming it all on you. "You don't turn me on anymore!" So while your spouse copes with all that, you develop your own feelings of unattractiveness, inadequacy, rejection, being unwanted, helplessness, and sexual dissatisfaction because he does not tell you the truth. But know this: your hubby's erectile dysfunction has nothing to do with you.

Most men associate their manhood with their sexual capabilities, so performance failure is devastating and demeaning to them. It robs them of their virility. Impotence can sometimes be more shattering than a jail term, terminal illness, or a close relative's passing. But then again, it is not difficult to see how an inability to function sexually affects a man's sense of value. In Joe's case, facing the reality remains his greatest challenge. However, his reaction represents that of the majority of men with erectile dysfunction. They cannot get themselves to admit they suffer from it. Somehow, therefore, someone needs to intervene to have the truth out in the open, so the problem can be addressed. Perhaps, this is where the wife comes in . . . or, as in Joe's case, a close friend like Dan comes in.

Nourishing a Healthy Perspective about Sex

Research shows that sex has many great benefits. It has been found to lower stress and blood pressure while boosting immunity. Sex once or twice a week has been linked with higher levels of antibodies (called immunoglobulin), which can protect you from colds and other infections. It is also good for the brain because it releases endorphins that decrease stress and induce a state of euphoria. It also boosts your body's oxytocin, which enhances your body's painkillers for fighting headaches and arthritis, even PMS. Sex also increases your lifespan. There are many more pluses to sex and sexual fulfilment that I cannot even begin to capture here. Bottom line: sex is very good for you, so anything that hinders your enjoyment of it in marriage should be sorted out.

When you embrace sex without inhibitions, unrealistic expectations, fear, or guilt, it is fun, exciting, and enjoyable. This God-given gift can be fulfilling only within the parameters of safety and freedom, which is why it is the ultimate celebration of marriage. Besides physical pleasure and unity, sex also brings emotional and spiritual wholeness. God intended it to provide a divine connection between you and your spouse.

Lack of communication about sexual problems and the absence of caring can tear your marriage apart. Do not wait several months to talk about intimacy issues with your spouse because it hurts your relationship. No matter what ups and downs you experience as a couple, have an open line of communication, founded on a nonthreatening, unbiased approach. Be patient, understanding, and caring towards each other because it is necessary. It is also important to be gentle, kind, and patient towards your man as he gets his act together.

If the cause is physical, seek medical help. If psychological, find a professional therapist.

Can romance exist without sex? Yes, it certainly can. Couples that have less or no sex do not necessarily have a loveless marriage because their intimacy can happen at the intellectual, emotional, spiritual, and recreational levels. If you have such a relationship, for as long as you both remain open and honest about your needs and feelings, your bond can still thrive. However, I do agree that a marriage without sex may be more vulnerable to infidelity. Do not withhold sex from your partner. If you must, you both must agree to it and it should last for only a short while. If your partner's sexual urges are greater than yours, find a middle ground. Compromise is the keyword here.

"The Song of Solomon" is THE book in the Bible for lovers. It details useful, vibrant romance, even without sex. The first chapter begins with a picture of very deep intimacy: "Let him kiss me with the kisses of his mouth." And it continues to illustrate how love encompasses all the senses: "your love is more delightful [sweeter] than wine", "pleasing is the fragrance of your perfumes", etc. I recommend that you read its chapters. Learn that words speak volumes even in the absence of physical intimacy.

Good sex takes effort and creativity. Each couple is unique in their style, desires, and levels of fulfilment. While chemistry has a great role in your sex life, health, age, and lifestyle play a major part in the fulfilment. Your busy life and high levels of stress can take their toll on you, so here are some tips that might help you:

1. Acknowledge that relationships are not static; growth is inevitable.

2. Work on your relationship purposefully by understanding your partner's needs.
3. Have a weekly scheduled sex date and warm up to it. Change the venue every now and then.
4. Surprise your partner with new energy and enthusiasm.
5. Do not criticise your partner, no matter what.
6. Practice love in action.

The need for sex and intimacy is regardless of gender and age. It is all a matter of attitude. You can enjoy sexual intimacy for a long time, even into your seventies and beyond. At your later stages in life, it has more depth because of your self-awareness, self-confidence, and lessons learned—and because you have less distractions to deal with. Sure, you do not have your youthful energies anymore, but that should not stop you. While you are both still young, have all the sex you want and need. Here are additional tips for your maximum enjoyment of sex:

1. Maintain good physical and psychological health.
2. Increase your intake of certain foods, e.g., broccoli, tomatoes, and pomegranate juice, because they boost your energies.
3. Give more affection, attention, and appreciation.
4. Structure quality time with your partner and be creative about it, e.g., couple's massage therapy.
5. Stay active. The more you do, the better it gets.
6. Remain faithful to your partner and keep the matrimonial bed pure.

Whatever happens, do not quit on intimacy. Continue to cuddle and touch. Use positive affirmations: admire, affirm, and appreciate. Be sensual, not sexual. Bottom line: erectile dysfunction is not the end of the road for your sex life as a couple.

> ## Reflection
>
> *4 Love is patient, love is kind. It does not envy, it does not boast, it is not proud. 5 It does not dishonor others, it is not self-seeking, it is not easily angered, it keeps no record of wrongs. 6 Love does not delight in evil but rejoices with the truth. 7 It always protects, always trusts, always hopes, always perseveres. 8 love never fails. (1st Corinthians 13. 4-8)*
>
> *18 May your fountain be blessed, and may you rejoice in the wife of your youth (Proverbs 5:18 - NIV)*

Chapter Nine

Worse Than Soap Opera

Jasper is sure of three things as far as his marriage is concerned. One, he loves his wife dearly. Two, he cannot picture a life without her. Three, he has no idea how to keep his marriage alive.

Jasper had married late because he could not seem to find the right girl. Whenever a potential candidate came up in his radar, he could not get hold of the time to settle down. He was always moving from one deal to the next, trying to earn as many shillings as he possibly could.

One day, Jasper's best friend invited him for coffee and told him to expect a surprise. When they met that afternoon, Jasper saw that Paul was with a beautiful young lady. His buddy quickly introduced them to each other. "I believe you both need to get acquainted. I will now leave you alone. My work here is done." Without giving the two a chance to respond, Paul got up and left.

Jasper and Flo indeed got to know each other that day. They parted ways, promising to meet again the very next afternoon. For the first time in his life, Jasper had met a woman he felt deeply for and whom he could imagine living with forever. They saw each other frequently over the succeeding weeks. Every time they did, he became more certain about his feelings. Not long afterwards, he was in for another surprise. When he turned up for their nth coffee date, he found Flo sullen and on edge. When asked about her mood, she flew off the handle.

Chapter Nine

"It's been weeks since we began doing this. What's going on? What are your plans? I don't want you to waste my time."

Flo's outburst caught Jasper unprepared, not so much because of what she said but how she said it. She was visibly upset and angling for a fight. Coming after less than two months of knowing each other, the confrontation was a bit unsettling for Jasper. Still, he tried to explain his plans, which calmed her down. The very sweet woman he had known in the past six weeks returned and they enjoyed what was left of the evening. However, Jasper could not forget the image of an angry woman from his mind.

Soon after, Jasper and Flo got married, and she moved in with him. She was an excellent housekeeper. In a very short time, she had managed to transform his bachelor pad into a beautiful home. She supervised the washing and ironing of his clothes by a house help, but she cooked his meals herself. She appeared very tender and loving, until something upset her. When that happened, she became unpredictable.

Having been a long-time bachelor, Jasper was used to living without being answerable to anybody. He came and went as he wished. It did not take long for that particular habit of his to become a battleground. He regularly received calls from Flo after work, asking his whereabouts and time of arrival. Barely half an hour later, she would phone him again. She did not stop until he actually walked through the doorway of their home.

One day, he needed to meet his friends for a drink. As usual, Flo's calls kept coming and interrupting their conversation. Irritated, Jasper switched off his phone and did not come home until shortly before midnight. He came upon a war zone when he arrived. His leather couch had been slashed. Plates had been smashed. Most of his suits had been ripped apart. Enraged, Jasper walked into the bedroom to find his wife waiting for him. She admitted to causing the damage but blamed him for making her angry. Although usually a very controlled individual, Jasper lost his cool that night. He ordered Flo to put her stuff together and he dropped her off at her sister's house. All the way, she begged him for forgiveness and promised never to do that again, but he would hear none of it.

Weeks later, Jasper began to miss her. Meantime, their mutual friends sent him messages about how remorseful Flo was and how much she missed him. In time, his heart softened, so they met and talked things over. They decided to give each other a second chance and everything seemed to be better indeed. But that lull did not last forever.

One day, Flo turned up at his office, unannounced. She was in the vicinity, so she decided to buy him lunch, drop it off, and go home. Because the receptionist did not know her, Flo was made to wait for a long time, lumped up together with all the business visitors. After more than half an hour, she got up, swept past the receptionist, and rushed to Jasper's office. In front of a very important client, she lectured her husband about not letting "that prostitute" make her wait. She punctuated her tirade by flinging items from her husband's desk across the room. Jasper had her forcefully removed from the building. He also took her house keys away from her. After work, he drove straight home, boxed up all her possessions, and left them outside the door, hoping she would get the message.

And then a new cycle started: He forgot. She begged. He missed her. She promised to change. He took her back in. She misbehaved. He threw her out. It went on and on with no end or real change in sight.

Chapter Nine

Behind the Drama

Flo is a classic example of a drama queen, an attention-seeking woman with a tendency to create chaos as a way of dealing with situations that cause her offence, pain, disappointment, or frustration. A few minutes with a drama queen (or king, if a man) can leave you in need of a painkiller or a long drive anywhere far from her. When allowed to get away with her actions for extended periods, someone like Flo can develop an addictive habit of whiny, nagging, disruptive, and destructive drama. Psychiatrist Judith Orloff describes a drama queen (implies drama king as well from this point on) as an "energy vampire". She warns that drama queens and kings are more widespread than you think.

Are you or someone you know a drama queen? The characteristics are plain for all to see. The drama queen overreacts to simple setbacks or imagined slights. Her life seems to be filled constantly with tragedy, bad luck, negativity, and chaos. Does this describe you? If so, then you certainly qualify for the title. If it portrays somebody else you know, then read on and find ways of dealing with her.

Initially, drama is your way of dealing with life's challenges and frustrations. As time goes by, this method of responding to circumstances can turn from a simple reaction to an emotional and physiological addiction, which demands to be satisfied. Addiction specialist Dr Howard Westman explains that the drama queen's antics can sometimes be more than just random acts of a girl gone wild. According to him, the attention you crave actually increases pleasure receptors in your brain. As in any addiction, your desire for this feeling can cause you to seek out hardship and trouble in your life, so you can react dramatically and experience pleasure.

Your childhood experience can also be a factor to your craving for drama. Through a traumatic episode, you may have discovered that dramatic behaviour gets you the attention you need. After years of using this method to gain notice, you see anxiety and stress as normal, while peace and quiet frighten you or feel unnatural. Without a crisis, you are left bored and empty, so you tend to create a spectacle to reestablish the routine.

Regardless of the origins of your drama queen status, without doubt, the chaos and negativity you create adversely affect other people's and your emotional and physical health, productivity, and relationships. Drama can drive good people out of your life, leaving you to fill your life with more disorder.

The Relationship of Drama and Anger

Where there is drama, anger is never far behind. On its own, anger is a standard emotion with a wide range of intensity, from mild irritation to full-blown destructive rage. It is your reaction to a perceived threat. It can be caused by both external and internal events. Different people react to it in various ways. Some suppress it, while others either convert it into something else or redirect it towards people or things, which have nothing to do with its trigger. When not properly managed, anger can cause opportunistic illness; hypertension, depression, and many other ailments including cancer. Directed outwards, as in Flo's case, it can destroy everything in sight. Literally. Because anger is the primary expression of your frustrations, you seriously threaten all your relationships.

Chapter Nine

While the control and management of your anger are vital, it is equally important to deal with the underlying issues that tend to set it off. One such cause is baggage from your past. Previous hurts can become emotional volcanoes. When confronted with a threat, you can erupt, hurting yourself and others in the process. Your prior baggage makes it difficult for you to enter into meaningful relationships.

Sometimes, you not only carry with you a lot of baggage but also use it to justify unacceptable behaviour. It may help you to listen to and reflect upon what others say about you. Pay attention to the issues that constantly come up. You may then realise that your actions actually stem not from the present but the past. Have you been exposed to any physical or emotional abuse before? Are you ashamed of an experience? Reflect upon this because it may provide you the answer to your dilemma. Acknowledge and take charge of your conduct.

The ability to recognise and acknowledge the presence of a problem is key to your therapy. Your self-awareness is the first step towards your wellness and wholeness. If you have unresolved issues that hinder your present joy, pursue their resolution and use your past experiences as a learning opportunity. If you resist a confrontation with your past, it may be because you desire to wear the victim tag and to carry sympathy from others. Do yourself a favour and recognise that you need to change your mindset. Your traumatic past is unfortunate, but you should know that no one wants to be around an emotionally unhealthy person.

Are You Addicted to Drama?

Regardless of what generates it, drama can become an addiction, which can imprison you and its recipient, which, in the context of this book, may be your spouse. Just as there are people who cannot deal with a drama-less life, there are individuals who feel abnormal if drama is not created around them.

Below is a list of questions you should try to answer truthfully. If you answer yes to any of the questions, there is a good chance you are indeed addicted to drama in your life:

1. Do you dominate conversations by talking about yourself and your experiences constantly?
2. Do you tend to be negative, critical, or judgemental?
3. Are you always eager to talk about your problems to anyone who listens?
4. Have you ever tried to show others that you have suffered worse than they have in terms of pain and tragedies?
5. Do you repeatedly find yourself in relationships that are bad for you?
6. Do you find yourself attracted to people whose lives need fixing?
7. Do you handle stress by throwing tantrums?
8. Do you exaggerate the extent of your problems?
9. Do you look for drama in the lives of others?
10. Do you host pity parties for yourself?

Human beings are social creatures and need social interaction, feedback, and validation. If you are an emotionally mature person, you receive such essentials naturally from your daily life, e.g., your work and your stable relationships. However, if you are emotionally immature, you have low levels of self-esteem and self-confidence, so you tend to feel insecure. You counter your insecurity by spending a large portion of your time to the creation of situations in which you become the centre of attention.

Surprisingly, attention-seeking behaviour is common. Being the centre of attention alleviates feelings of insecurity and inadequacy. Unfortunately, the relief is temporary because the underlying problems—low self-confidence and low self-esteem, which result in decreased levels of self-worth and self-love—remain unaddressed. If you are insecure and emotionally immature, you often exhibit bullying behaviour as well, especially involving manipulation and deception. Bullies and harassers have the emotional age of a child. They throw temper tantrums, deceive, lie, and manipulate to avoid exposure of their true nature and to evade accountability and sanctions.

Be the Change You Need

When you lose your spouse and other loved ones because of your hot-headedness, at some point, you have to understand that you are their common problem. If you want your life to change, then you must initiate it yourself. Take responsibility; control your situation. Keep track of your emotional reactions and triggers. Ask your spouse to help keep you aware of your behaviour. Give them permission to tell you when you overreact, get dramatic, or become too negative.

Get help from a therapist, life coach, or counsellor to address the root causes of your addiction to drama and to suggest healthy coping strategies. You should also exercise impulse control. Learn to wait before reacting to any situation. It takes time to recalibrate and rewire your brain, but stick to your resolve. By "counting to ten" before saying or doing anything, you curtail your negative reactions.

Be patient with yourself and use humour to lighten tense moments. Practice being peaceful. If it works for you, spend time in natural settings because they promote peace and enable you to dial down your anxiety and stress. Do not let yourself fall into boredom; you can end up filling the void with drama . . . again. Instead, fill your life with positive activities and positive people. Limit your contact with other drama queens and provocative people. Set clear boundaries with them and try to redirect them positively yourself. Channel your energies into productive outlets. Engage in sports, fulfilling hobbies, etc.

Handling a Drama Queen/King

If you know outright or suspect your spouse is a drama king (stands for queen as well), then the guidelines listed below can help you deal with your partner:

Realise you are not the problem. The drama king is prone to place blame on others and not himself. Do not buy into the lie. Do not enable him by believing his accusations. It is bad for you and for him because it allows him to make you feel guilty and to enslave you to his whims without liberating him from the real problem.

Know that he will try anything to get what he wants. A drama king's philosophy is very simple: there is no such thing as bad attention. If with being nice to read If being nice does not give him what he wants, he can try the opposite, including picking a fight with you. In other words, he will do all he can to be the centre of attention.

Do not engage in his tantrums. He will throw a fit whenever something does not go his way, so be prepared to deal with tantrums. The best thing to do is ignore them. Walk away. Do not let him pull you back into the situation. If he attacks you in some way, say and do nothing. A drama king hates being ignored.

Express your displeasure. Tell him that you do not like his behaviour. Let him know in no uncertain terms that you will not tolerate his drama. Explain to him that you will terminate the relationship, if things continue as they are.

Steps for Getting Rid of Drama

Communicate. Different couples approach conflict differently. Some slug it out; others give each other the silent treatment. Whatever your approach, allow for a cooling-off period and then find a way to express your feelings. Give your spouse a similar opportunity and do not judge or belittle his emotions.

Approach each conflict with empathy. Put yourself in your spouse's shoes and understand that he has emotional wounds to deal with as well. The pain he causes you is real, but the reason he brings drama into your relationship is also a real hurt for him.

Listen. Listening is more than just hearing your spouse's words. You have to hear his feelings in them as well. Take turns talking and listening to each other without interruptions. If necessary, allot time limits, so you both have equal talk and listen intervals.

Seek healthy compromises. Conflict resolution is not fault-finding. When discussions revolve around assigning blame, nothing gets solved. The goal should be to resolve your differences, so that you both can come out ahead.

Forgive. Forgiveness is not a one-off decision. It is a journey and a process that takes time, determination, and persistence. Forgiveness is not forgetting. It is keeping pain from controlling your life. Forgiveness is not the same thing as excusing abusive behaviour or staying with an abuser. It means not paying back hurt for hurt. Being unforgiving leads to an accumulation of anger, which can harm you emotionally and physically. Forgiveness is not something you offer the drama queen/king of your life; it is a gift to yourself and your marriage.

Reflection

Then they cried out to the Lord in their trouble and He brought them out of their distress. He stilled the storm to a whisper; the waves of the sea were hushed. They were glad when it grew calm and He guided them to their desired haven. (Psalm 107:28-30)

Search me, God, and know my heart; test me and know my anxious thoughts. See if there is any offensive way in me and lead me in the way everlasting. (Psalm 139:23-24)

Chapter Ten

The Woman in His Mind

The first time Debra heard it, she thought she had imagined the whole thing. Did her husband moan another woman's name during their lovemaking? For the next several days, she turned the thought over and over again in her mind. Part of her was convinced Tony had called her Becky. Another part of her was not so sure. Her situation was made more difficult because they actually had a very happy marriage. Communication was good. Love was freely expressed. Trust had not been violated. Tony had never given her reason to doubt his faithfulness to her.

Debra was tempted to bring it up with her husband just to clear the air, but she did not know how to ease the topic into their conversation. What if he flew into a rage at the insinuation of an infidelity on his side? In the end, she decided to do nothing about it. However, it did not take long before the whole thing began to affect her relationship with Tony. She started to do things she had never done before: She sneaked into his phone to check his call logs and to read his messages. She watched her husband closely, reading his body language for any tell-tale signs of cheating. She found none. What was most affected, however, was their lovemaking. She could not enjoy herself fully because she listened for her husband to slip up and say another woman's name again. He never did, so she was left with a suspicion she could not prove and a lingering guilt at suspecting her husband for nothing.

In time, her concerns wore off and she concluded that her ears had played tricks on her. But her peace did not last long. Shortly after she dismissed the whole thing, it happened again. Tony blurted out the name Becky during their lovemaking. This time, she was sure and confronted him right then and there. Instead of denying it, he fell silent. Debra waited patiently, but her heart and mind were in turmoil. Finally, he spoke.

Tony reassured Debra that he had no desire to be with anybody else and that he loved her. However, he did confess that, one day, he had accidentally clicked on a Web link that led to a porn site. After that incident, he visited it several more times in the course of two weeks. Because his own guilt had eaten at him, he finally decided to stop. He never went back to the site again. Just the same, the damage had obviously been done. Tony developed sexual fantasies that found their way into intimate moments with his wife. For a while, he persuaded himself that they were harmless because they involved a complete stranger. If anything, they seemed to enhance his sexual experience, but deep down in his heart, he knew that they could—and did—hurt Debra.

The Truth about Porn

Who would have ever thought that porn would come this far today? Years ago, when I was growing up, it was something that was available only through magazines like *Playboy* and *Penthouse*. Nowadays, you can visit thousands of websites and watch hours of porn videos from anywhere in the world. Many individuals develop porn addiction and consequently lose interest in their own sexual relationships.

Pornography is the presentation of sexual subject matter for the purpose of sexual arousal. It may be presented in a variety of print publications and is easily available on DVDs and the like or via the Internet. Today, many people are addicted to it. Like online gambling, porn addiction is easy to fall into because it takes only the click of a button to immerse yourself in seductive images. Because of its availability and accessibility—in the comfort of your own private space and via this generation's ubiquitous gadget, the mobile phone—it is all the more devastating to individual lives and relationships.

How can you tell if you or your spouse is addicted to porn? If you view it for hours and feel powerless to stop. If it affects your work, social life, sleep, or concentration. If you feel it controls you. Porn blunts your senses and leaves you unable to focus on anything else. It can also leave you feeling disgusted with yourself. Excessive porn viewing steals time away from real life and potentially productive projects.

If porn addiction is a problem in your marriage, the best way to address it is to understand how it begins and grows. Below are the five stages of porn addiction:

1. **Early Exposure**. Most porn addicts are exposed to the material while still young. Their youthful curiosity keeps them glued to sex.
2. **Addiction.** In time, curiosity becomes an addiction they cannot control. They find themselves going back to porn repeatedly. It becomes a part of their lives. At this point, they are hooked and cannot pull away from its allure.
3. **Escalation.** As the addiction progresses, their desire for porn escalates. They start to look for more graphic sex videos and images, which they used to shun and

be disgusted at in the beginning. Previously loathed materials become exciting and thrilling to them.

4. **Desensitisation.** Eventually, porn addicts start to become numb even to the most explicit porn they could get their hands on. Nothing stimulates them anymore. The desire for the thrill is as strong as before, but they cannot find anything to satisfy their lust.

5. **Acting Out Sexually.** They take the images from screen and paper to their real-world experiences. They desire to enact what is presented in those media.

According to Tony, when he reached Stage Five, he had already started fantasising about sex with the woman on the site. That is how he ended up calling out Becky's name during his lovemaking with Debra.

Sexual fantasies are considered taboo, so your spouse may not admit to indulging in them. He may also not disclose their nature lest he be judged as weird, wrong, or even perverse. His fantasies may be triggered by a person or an object, and they are phenomena similar to dreams. Some sexual fantasies are gratifying and enjoyable, while others may cause unsettling thoughts and psychological challenges. According to Freudian psychoanalysts, they happen as a means of satisfying your wish or conquering your memories of traumatic personal experiences.

Arousal is crucial in sexual enjoyment and the mind plays a major role in achieving it. When your thoughts dwell on work, negativity, or other unromantic subjects during lovemaking, you cannot achieve sexual satisfaction. Instead of these, fill your head with memories of the best sexual moments with your spouse, plans for your next sexy times, and similar thoughts. Commit to becoming more spontaneous and generous in bed to keep the flame alive.

Rather than letting fantasies rule over you, take charge of your thoughts. Control is necessary because thoughts are not always reliable, edifying, or good. If you obsess over sexual fantasies with someone other than your spouse, you erode your intimacy and, consequently, can ruin the relationship.

How to Overcome Porn Addiction

The greatest gift to yourself when recovering from addiction is to love yourself. Do what you have to do to recover your life. To quit porn, you have to drop your ego and go through the arduous recovery process. Be honest about all your desires, especially the deepest, darkest ones related to your addiction. Vulnerability is the first step towards loving yourself as a person and also the toughest to practice.

In counselling, a major element to consider is your free will. You always have a choice. You can undo the effects of your childhood exposure to porn. You can train yourself to make different decisions that are actually positive. One way to start is reminding yourself that you are not your addiction. You can challenge the suggestions of your mind.

You or your loved one may be stuck at that point where you confuse sex with intimacy. The pathway to healing involves redefining intimacy. Here is how you find your way out of porn addiction:

1. **Acknowledge the addiction.** Do not deny the problem. *Whoever conceals their sins does not prosper, but the one who confesses and renounces them finds mercy.* (Proverbs 28:31)

2. **Recognise that what you are doing is wrong.** Do not justify your addiction in any way. *For everything in the world—the lust of the flesh, the lust of the eyes, and the pride of life—comes not from the Father but from the world.* (1 John 2:16)

3. **Do not blame others.** Take responsibility for your actions. The addiction begins and ends with you. *Why do you look at the speck of sawdust in your brother's eye and pay no attention to the plank in your own eye?* (Matthew 7:3)

4. **Be accountable to a spiritual authority.** Have a safe person to share your struggles with. *Therefore confess your sins to each other and pray for each other so that you may be healed. The prayer of a righteous person is powerful and effective.* (James 5:16)

5. **Recognise that willpower is not the answer.** Admit that you need God's help, so you can open up your life to His supernatural intervention. When you yield to His will, He can transform you. *But seek first His kingdom and His righteousness and all these things will be given to you as well.* (Matthew 6:33)

6. **Study God's Word regarding sexual purity.** Immerse yourself in Scripture, so He can guide you better. *Therefore, get rid of all moral filth and the evil that is so prevalent and humbly accept the word planted in you, which can save you.* (James 1:21)

7. **Destroy any and all forms of porn in your possession.** Do not hide anything. Do not keep anything. You cannot wean yourself off pornography. This is one addiction that you must quit cold turkey. *Flee*

the evil desires of youth and pursue righteousness, faith, love, and peace, along with those who call on the Lord out of a pure heart. (2 Timothy 2:22)

8. **Flee from temptation.** Do not play with fire. Do not bring yourself in close proximity to porn. *Do not set foot on the path of the wicked or walk in the way of evildoers. Avoid it; do not travel on it; turn from it and go on your way.* (Proverbs 4:14-15)

9. **Give yourself time to recover.** Anticipate that you still have a long process ahead of you. It may be painful, but persevere. Victory over addiction is achieved in a marathon, not a sprint. "... I am the Lord who heals you." (Exodus 15:26)

10. **Live a day at a time.** Celebrate daily achievements. Rejoice in your progress.

How to Recover from Your Spouse's Porn Addiction

When Debra found out about Tony's porn addiction, a sense of betrayal overwhelmed her. She was more in shock than angry; the experience had numbed her. One day, her marriage seemed normal; the next day, it was not. She had no clue how to find her way out and was unprepared for the crushing pain. What was the way forward for her? Debra's own journey of recovery began with prayer and counselling. After that foundation is set, you can follow the path she took with these steps:

Understand male sexuality. When your husband turns to porn for sexual pleasure, it is common to blame yourself for it. DO NOT. It has nothing to do with your physical appearance or your bedroom behaviour. It is all about him and his issues. One thing you should know: he does love you. He is actually ashamed of his behaviour. He needs your love and support. It may be helpful to find and read literature about his sexuality, so you can comprehend his impulses and motivations.

Amplify your role as helpmate. Your role is to support your husband as you grow in unity with each other and in closeness with God. Of course, your motives are everything. If your motive is love, you will give him unconditional acceptance and help him get back on his feet again. Speak in calmness. Affirm him as much as possible. How you treat him determines the quality of his healing and recovery from addiction.

Focus on other people and things. When you focus your attention on your personal challenges, you magnify it out of proportion. Distract your mind from the issues by looking out for others. Or keep yourself busy with hobbies, e.g., gardening, tutoring, visiting the sick, etc. Do not hold pity parties.

Focus on God and His Word. With God, nothing is impossible. His promises deal with all aspects of your life: health, relationships, finances, family, work, love, and so on. Search God's Word to find His promises and hold onto them. Thank Him for them. Whenever you speak God's promises into your life, you make their reality draw near. Whenever you thank Him for them, you remain in His will even when it seems very hard.

Debra began to memorise Scripture. She ensured that she had some in the car to remember while caught up in traffic. She started praying daily and claiming healing for her husband and herself. She allowed God to transform her mind, attitude, and relationships. While at home, she also had verses on sticky notes posted all over the house. In other words, be creative and fill your mind with positive words to heal your heart.

Never to Return Again

It is important at this point that you and your spouse set new boundaries, recommit your love and dedication to your marriage, and chart ways of holding each other accountable. Whatever else happens, uphold honesty as your highest value. Most sexually addicted people lie to themselves and their partners, so do not create situations where your spouse cannot be truthful to you. The more honest and open he becomes, the more included you feel. When this happens, you can become a team, fighting together against the addiction, not against each other. Evaluate your mutual progress weekly, monthly, and quarterly and reward yourselves for staying on track.

As you struggle along the path of recovery, remember that his action has nothing to do with your attractiveness or desirability. Whatever you do, do not turn inward to find fault with yourself. Instead, discover ways to support your spouse. Healing is possible. If you both are willing, you can use your struggle as an opportunity to draw closer to each other. Your bond can become stronger as you each play your role to encourage, support, affirm, and inspire one another. By God's grace, you can create a marriage built to last.

Reflection

No temptation[a] has overtaken you except what is common to mankind. And God is faithful; he will not let you be tempted[b] beyond what you can bear. But when you are tempted,[c] he will also provide a way out so that you can endure it.
(1 Corinthians 10:13)

1. *Have mercy on me, O God,*
   according to your unfailing love;
   according to your great compassion
   blot out my transgressions.

2. *Wash away all my iniquity*
   and cleanse me from my sin.

3. *For I know my transgressions,*
   and my sin is always before me.

4. *Against you, you only, have I sinned*
   and done what is evil in your sight;
   so you are right in your verdict
   and justified when you judge.

5. *Surely I was sinful at birth,*
   sinful from the time my mother conceived me.

6. *Yet you desired faithfulness even in the womb;*
   you taught me wisdom in that secret place.

7. *Cleanse me with hyssop, and I will be clean;*
   wash me, and I will be whiter than snow.

8. *Let me hear joy and gladness;*
   let the bones you have crushed rejoice.

9. *Hide your face from my sins*
   and blot out all my iniquity.

10. *Create in me a pure heart, O God,*
    and renew a steadfast spirit within me.

11. *Do not cast me from your presence*
    or take your Holy Spirit from me.

12. *Restore to me the joy of your salvation*
    and grant me a willing spirit, to sustain me.

(Psalm 51 1-12)

Conclusion

Congratulations on finishing this book! I hope you found encouragement and support as you read through the chapters. I know that healing beyond betrayal is no walk in the park. Some days, it feels impossible. But remember this: the pain will recede in time.

Betrayal is probably the most devastating thing you can experience. When your spouse deceives you, your trust is lost. Your world crumbles. When betrayal happens to you, you realise fearfully that the other person has the capacity to hurt you immensely. You awaken to a new reality: you are just as vulnerable as everybody else, when it comes to betrayal.

Betrayal is a violation of your trust and goodwill. It produces moral and psychological conflicts within your relationship. It can be a result of broken promises, failed loyalties, unfaithfulness, or unmet expectations. It has destroyed marriages, ended long-term friendships, and created havoc in families, causing everybody involved a lot of pain, frustration, anger, stress, and depression. Whether the deception is committed by your spouse, you experience an affliction that takes a long time to heal. Some, in fact, never recover.

Healing from betrayal involves teamwork. You and your spouse must be fully committed to rebuilding your marriage. More importantly, you both need to establish mechanisms to ensure that it never happens again.

Ultimately, the key to healing from betrayal is forgiveness. If your spouse had betrayed you, you must find a way to forgive

Conclusion

him. If you are the offending party, you must learn to forgive yourself and seek forgiveness. Forgiveness reopens the door to true intimacy and connection. It results from a conscious decision to stop the blame game, make peace, and start afresh on a clean slate. If the past has had you in its clutches, take the next step to have more love in your life: decide to forgive today.

Trust is also crucial in your marriage. It is cultivated over long periods but can be destroyed in the blink of an eye. It is a powerful tool that helps your relationship grow in every aspect. It builds a sense of security for you and your spouse. You can show it by never intentionally hurting your spouse in any way. Be gentle in your expressions of caring.

Acceptance is also important to a healthy, happy marriage. It is not easy for two people of completely different backgrounds to come together and share a home. It requires compromise and unconditional acceptance. Accept your spouse as he is. Do not waste your energies, trying to change him. No one is perfect, so acceptance means you do not hold your spouse's weaknesses against him. Focus on the qualities that made you fall in love with him in the first place. Remember your commitment: for richer or poorer, better or worse, in sickness and in health.

Communication is the foundation of a strong marital union. It is absolutely vital that you and your spouse learn how to have open and honest communication, if you want to have a successful, happy, and lasting marriage. Understanding what your spouse wants to hear comes by listening to him and understanding his personality. It is also essential to give your spouse clues about what you need. Many relationships

Conclusion

fail because of misunderstandings. Open communication skills are necessary if your relationship is to stay strong. If you sense that your spouse is disconnected or you are unhappy about something, do not ignore or turn a blind eye to the situation. Discuss and iron out the issues. You may be frustrated, angry, or hurt, and he may be, too, but your goal should be to resolve your differences. The only viable way of doing so is through open and direct communication.

Talk about This

1. What is your partner's and your natural response to your relationship challenges?
2. What key lessons have you learned about your relationship from this book?
3. What action plan do you have in place to find healing and prosperity in your relationship?
4. How do you evaluate to ensure accountability for your spouse and you?
5. If necessary, can you both agree to consider therapy or professional guidance?

Should you consider the last item, Anchor Relationship Network is available to help you. Visit www.jenniekarina.co.ke, for more details and to send immediate feedback about this book.

In all this, trust God and seek Him diligently.

> *Above all, love each other deeply because love covers over a multitude of sins.* (1 Peter 4:8)

References

Baldwin, David, and Sally Thomas. *Depression and Sexual Function*. London: Martin Dunitz, 1996.

Chapman, Gary. *The Five Love Languages: How to Express Heartfelt Commitment to Your Mate*. Sydney: Strand Publishing, 1992.

Covenant Eyes. "Get the Latest Pornography Statistics." Accessed March 11, 2015. http://www.covenanteyes.com/2013/02/19/pornography-statistics/.

Gregoire, Alaine, and John P. Pryor. *Impotence: An Integrated Approach to Clinical Practice*. Edinburgh: Churchill Livingstone, 1993.

Hendrix, Harville. *Getting the Love You Want: A Guide for Couples*. New York: Henry Holt & Co., 2008.

Karina, Jennifer. *Marriage Built to Last: After the Promise*. Nairobi: Integrity Publishers, 2011.

Lassri, Dana, and Golan Shahar. "Self-Criticism Mediates the Link between Childhood Emotional Maltreatment and Young Adults' Romantic Relationships." *Journal of Social and Clinical Psychology* 31.3 (2012): 289-311.

Metz, Michael E., and Barry W. McCarthy. *Coping With Erectile Dysfunction: How to Regain Confidence and Enjoy Great Sex*. Oakland, CA: New Harbinger Publications, 2004.

Olson, David H., and Amy K. Olson. *Empowering Couples: Building on Your Strengths*. Minneapolis, MN: Life Innovations, 2000.

Orloff, Judith. *Positive Energy: 10 Extraordinary Prescriptions for Transforming Fatigue, Stress & Fear into Vibrance, Strength & Love*. New York: Harmony Books, 2004.

References

Rosenberg, Morris, and Timothy J. Owens. "Low Self-Esteem People: A Collective Portrait." In *Extending Self-Esteem Theory and Research: Sociological and Psychological Currents*, edited by Timothy J. Owens, Sheldon Stryker, and Norman Goodman, 400-36. New York: Cambridge University Press, 2001.

Scientific American. "Dangerous Liaisons: How to Deal with a Drama Queen." Accessed March 11, 2015. http://www.scientificamerican.com/article/dangerous-liaisons/.

Secunda, Victoria. *Women and Their Fathers: The Sexual and Romantic Impact of the First Man in Your Life*. New York: Delacorte Press, 1992.

Sprecher, Susan, and Rodney M. Cate. "Sexual Satisfaction and Sexual Expression as Predictors of Relationship Satisfaction and Stability." In *The Handbook of Sexuality in Close Relationships*, edited by John H. Harvey, Amy Wenzel, and Susan Sprecher, 235-56. Mahwah, NJ: Lawrence Erlbaum Associates Publishers, 2004.

Tim Field Foundation. "Drama Queens, Saviours, Rescuers, Feigners, and Attention-Seekers: Attention-Seeking Personality Disorders, Victim Syndrome, Insecurity, and Centre of Attention Behaviour." Accessed March 11, 2015. http://www.bullyonline.org/workbully/attent.htm.

U.S. News & World Report. "Is Drama Queen (or King) a Real Diagnosis?" Accessed March 11, 2015. http://health.usnews.com/health-news/patient-advice/articles/2015/02/25/is-drama-queen-or-king-a-real-diagnosis.

Wetsman Forensic Medicine. Accessed March 11, 2015. http://townsendla.com.

About the Author

Jennifer Karina is an entrepreneur, motivational speaker, life coach, newspaper columnist, and author of the book, *Marriage Built to Last: After the Promise*. She is also the founder and CEO of Anchor Relationship Network. Jennifer is a director of various companies in both private and public sectors, and serves as Chief Commissioner of the Kenya Girl Guides Association. She has professional training in Business Administration and Counselling Psychology. She holds an MA from Durham University (UK) and is working on a PhD in Educational Psychology.

In February 2015, Jennifer received the Women Leadership Achievement Award at the World Women Leadership Congress in Mumbai, India. It is a global honour to celebrate outstanding women professionals with "the vision, flair, acumen, and professionalism to demonstrate excellent leadership and management skills in an organisation".

Jennifer has been married to Bob Karina for more than thirty years and is a mother of three married children. She has a total of eight grandchildren. She enjoys playing golf with her husband and spending quality time with her children and grandchildren. Jennifer also loves reading and writing. She is passionate about helping others build strong, lasting, and thriving relationships.

Get a copy today!

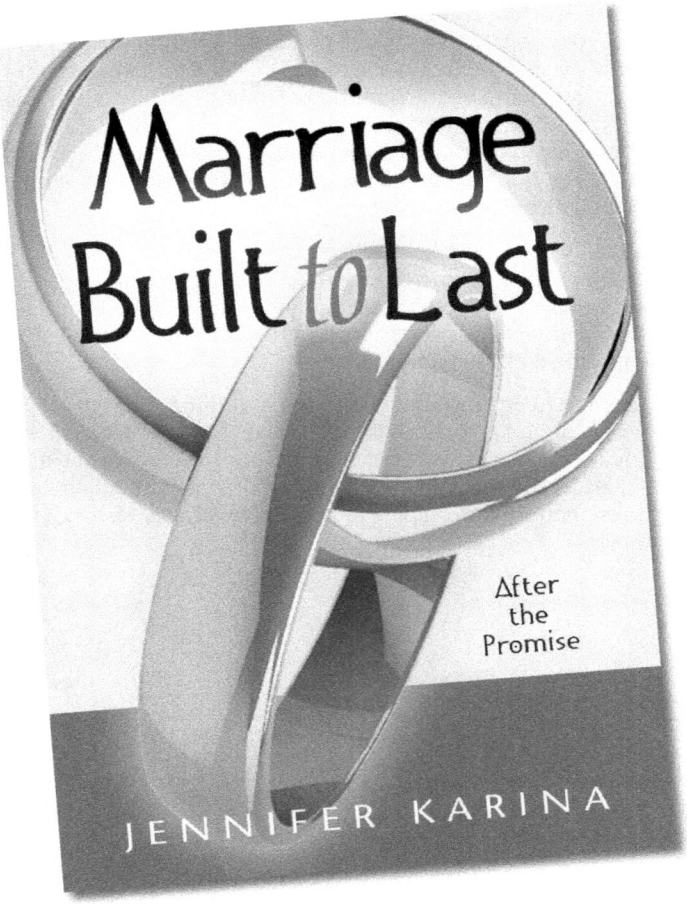

Order now.

Available at all leading bookstores in Nairobi, Kenya.
Order an autographed copy via www.jenniekarina.co.ke.

About *Marriage Built to Last: After the Promise*

This is the perfect book for me. Having experienced my fair share of broken marriages, I find *Marriage Built to Last* relevant, inspiring, and a great compass to help people navigate [their way through marriage]. Jennifer has a way of keeping her readers engaged and encouraged.

Wanja Southerland, *Nalley Toyota of Roswell Business Development Centre Consultant (Atlanta, GA, USA)*

It is a practical, humorous, and sensitive home-grown book, written by a Kenyan for Africans and the world. It is a useful guide for young people and couples determined to find and sustain a happy marriage. It is written from a Christian perspective with Biblical references for the modern, urban individual.

Dorothy Nyong'o, *7th Sense Communications, Ltd. Managing Director (Nairobi, Kenya)*

It is unlike other marriage books I have ever read. It combines foundational principles for marriage, motivational insights, and biblical teachings. The material is presented in engaging, concise prose, and provides excellent and relevant examples. This book will appeal not only to laypersons [getting into marriage or newly married] but also to the marriage veterans.

Dr Kirimi Barine, *Publishing Institute of Africa Founder-Director (Nairobi, Kenya)*

I greatly enjoyed reading it. My wife [uses] it as a course material for our marriage and family classes. We actually bought copies for our library.

Rev Thaiya Wallace, *Lighthouse Outreaches Mentor (Limuru, Kenya)*

It is a timely resource in helping address and resolve many questions and situations that you will encounter in your journey into and through marriage—from bedroom intimacy to raising children, from finances to forgiveness. It tackles real issues to ensure your marriage is built to last. It is written in a practical and down-to-earth style. You will find it at once delightful, insightful, and refreshing.

Bishop Allan and **Rev Kathy Kiuna**, *Jubilee Christian Church Founder and General Overseer, and Senior Associate Pastor (Nairobi, Kenya)*

Jennifer fuses her faith in God, life and family journeys, counselling skills, knowledge of God's word, and passion for a happy, fulfilling, and meaningful marriage. This book is filled with godly principles and practical ideas.

Pastor Elijah Wanje, *Ridgeways Baptist Church Senior Pastor (Nairobi, Kenya)*

My husband and I have used [the book] to mentor many couples. The book has been very useful and has made a big difference in our own marriage, family life, and [respective] personal growths. We highly recommend it to every couple that desires a lasting marriage.

Beatrice and **Douglas Wambua**, *Marriage and Family Life Mentors (Nairobi, Kenya)*

It addresses not only married couples but singles, too. It empowered me through the chapters on self-esteem and confidence, dating, and finding the right partner. It helped me examine myself, recognise relationships that needed to end, and improve my other [associations].

Tania Mwangi, *Student (Dallas, TX, USA)*

Contact

The author would appreciate your feedback through

Website: www.jenniekarina.co.ke

Email: jennie@karina.co.ke

Or

Anchor Relationship Network

P.O. Box 74858- 00200

Nairobi, Kenya

Cell: +254 707 633 433

+ 254 734 713 650

Email: lovelife@jenniekarina.co.ke

Visit www.jenniekarina.co.ke for additional resources such as individual reflection and group discussion questions.

www.ingramcontent.com/pod-product-compliance
Lightning Source LLC
Chambersburg PA
CBHW060807050426
42449CB00008B/1579